This Is Islam

From Muhammad and the Community of Believers
to Islam in the Global Community

Praise for the "This World of Ours" Series

This Fleeting World: A Short History of Humanity

I first became an avid student of David Christian by watching his course, Big History, *on DVD, and so I am very happy to see his enlightening presentation of the world's history captured in these essays. I hope it will introduce a wider audience to this gifted scientist and teacher.*

Bill Gates

No one except David Christian could do it. He has a unique talent for mastering data, processing it efficiently, and writing it up lucidly. He can simplify without dumbing down and can be provocative without sliding into outrage. Readers can rely on him for a sensitive, well-informed, well-judged, reflective, and miraculously concise overview.

Felipe Fernández-Armesto,
professor of modern history,
University of Notre Dame

This Is China: The First 5,000 Years

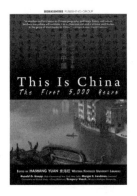

It is hard to imagine that such a short book can cover such a vast span of time and space. This Is China: The First 5,000 Years *will help teachers, students, and general readers alike, as they seek for a preliminary guide to the contexts and complexities of Chinese culture.*

Jonathan Spence,
professor of history,
Yale University; author of
The Search for Modern China

In this slim volume, tiny by comparison with its regiments of oversize competitors in the crowded field of general histories of China, a team of experts has performed the miracle of distilling their collective knowledge into a seamless and lucid essay on Chinese geography, prehistory, history, and culture.

Gregor Benton, Cardiff University

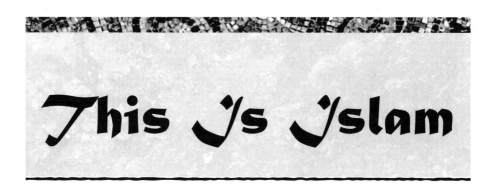

This Is Islam

From Muhammad and the Community of Believers to Islam in the Global Community

Jamal J. Elias

BERKSHIRE PUBLISHING GROUP
Great Barrington, Massachusetts

Published by:
Berkshire Publishing Group LLC
122 Castle Street
Great Barrington, Massachusetts 01230
www.berkshirepublishing.com

Printed in the United States of America

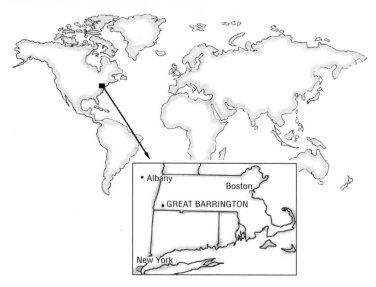

Library of Congress Cataloging-in-Publication Data
Elias, Jamal J.
    This is Islam : from Muhammad and the community of believers to Islam in the global community / Jamal J. Elias.
        p. cm. -- (This world of ours)
    Includes bibliographical references and index.
    ISBN 978-1-933782-81-2 (alk. paper) -- ISBN 978-1-933782-82-9 (electronic) 1. Islam. I. Title.
    1. World history. 2. Civilization—History. I. Title.
    BP161.3.E554 2010
    297--dc22   2010023974

Credits

Advisors

Amina Inloes, *Islamic College, London, U.K.*
Katherine Liss Saffle, *Heritage Hall Upper School*
Namji Steinemann, *East-West Center*
Laura Wangerin, *Latin School of Chicago*

Further thanks to

Kenneth Bernstein, *Eleanor Roosevelt High School;* **J. D. Bowers,** *Northern Illinois University;*
Susan Douglass, *George Mason University;* **Joshua Fahler,** *Clear Springs High School;*
Dale A. Hueber, *East Bay High School;* **John A. King, Jr.,** *Ransom Everglades School;*
Brandon Marriott, *University of Oxford;* **John Maunu,** *AP/Collegeboard World History*
consultant; **Timothy May,** *North Georgia College & State University;* **Barbara Petzen,** *Center*
for Middle Eastern Studies, Harvard University; **Tim Vermande,** *Art Institute of Indianapolis;*
Jane Weber, *Nashua Community College;* **Charles Weller,** *Asia Research Associates*

Editorial Staff

Mary Bagg, Rachel Christensen, Barbara Resch

Design and Production

Anna Myers, *Designer*
Newgen Imaging Systems, *Composition*
Thomson-Shore, Inc., *Printing*

Image Sources

Front cover, bottom: This detailed mosaic of a vase with an acanthus motif, found on the inner walls
of the Dome of the Rock shrine in Jerusalem, was created c. 690 CE during the rule of Sunni caliph
'Abd al-Mailk ibn Marwān. *10.000 Meisterwerke der Malerei,* Yorck Project.
Front cover, top: Skyline illustration by Anna Myers.
About the author: Photo by Mir Masud-Elias.
Back cover, inset: A calligraphic fragment from 1550 includes a maxim drawn from the *Munajat*
(Supplications) of the great Persian mystic and scholar Khwajah 'Abdallah Ansari (died 1088).
Library of Congress.
Illustrations:
Library of Congress.
Louvre Museum. Paris, France.
D. S. Margoliouth. (1905). *Mohammed and the Rise of Islam.* London: G. P. Putnam's Sons.
New York Public Library.
Pew Research Center's Forum on Religion & Public Life (http://pewforum.org/).
Jane M. Sawyer (morguefile.com).
Yale University Library.
M. J. B. Silvestre, (1850). *Universal Palaeography: or, Fac-Similes of Writings of All Nations and Periods*
(Frederic Madden, Trans.) London: Henry Bohn.

Contents

Publisher's Note xi

Teachers' Preface xvii

What Is Islam? 1

Arabs and Arabia before Islam 5

Muhammad and the Emergence of Islam 9

Islamic Texts 19

Islamic Sects 29

Philosophy and Theology 53

Teachings 63

The Mosque and Prayer 79

Islamic Rites 85

Islamic Law 99

Challenges of the Modern Era 107

Resources 113

Index 117

About the Author 125

Publisher's Note

his Is Islam is the third book in a series of short historical companions from Berkshire Publishing Group, but its original draft preceded those of the other two books by ten years. Jamal J. Elias was the chair of the Religion Department at Amherst College at that time, and he wrote a chapter for a book that was never published. (He is now chair of the Department of Religious Studies at the University of Pennsylvania.) His manuscript lingered in our files, and in my mind. His description of the early years of Islam, and especially of its incredibly rapid spread, is one of the stories that helped me see that the past was far more dynamic and vital, and that the people in the past were far more mobile, than I had ever realized.

This was about the same time that Berkshire began to specialize in world history with the help of historians like William H. McNeill and David Christian. As we worked on the second edition of the *Berkshire Encyclopedia of World History*, winner of *Library Journal* Best Reference Source 2004, *Booklist* Editor's Choice 2004, and *Choice* Outstanding Academic Title 2004, we began to look for other areas of history, important in the world today and too little understood, that we could present in compact books like this one.

One afternoon, while I was leafing through a magazine story, Jamal Elias's piece came to mind. It turned out to be the right length for a short book, and with his help and the help of a remarkable group of teachers and scholars who offered advice in response to Listserv postings, we have reworked the original manuscript. We have also added new material, including poems, photographs, maps, and thought-provoking sidebars, to create this succinct and compelling introduction to a religion that has shaped nations and regions, as well as individual lives.

Karen Christensen 沈凯伦
CEO, Berkshire Publishing Group 宝库山, Great Barrington, Massachusetts

Distribution of Muslim Population by Country

Only countries with more than 1 million Muslims are shown

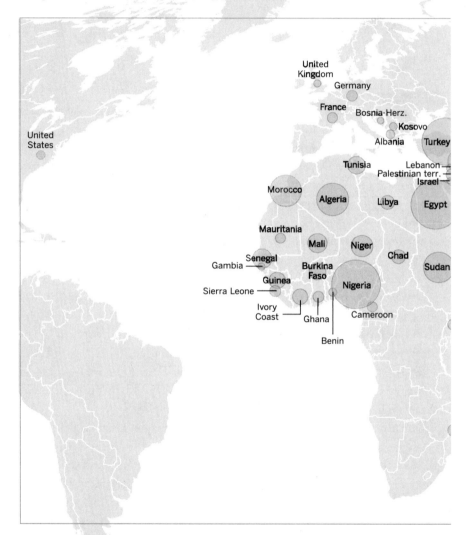

United Kingdom
Germany
France
Bosnia-Herz.
Kosovo
Albania
Turkey
United States
Tunisia
Lebanon
Palestinian terr.
Israel
Morocco
Algeria
Libya
Egypt
Mauritania
Mali
Niger
Chad
Sudan
Senegal
Gambia
Burkina Faso
Guinea
Nigeria
Sierra Leone
Ivory Coast
Ghana
Cameroon
Benin

and Territory

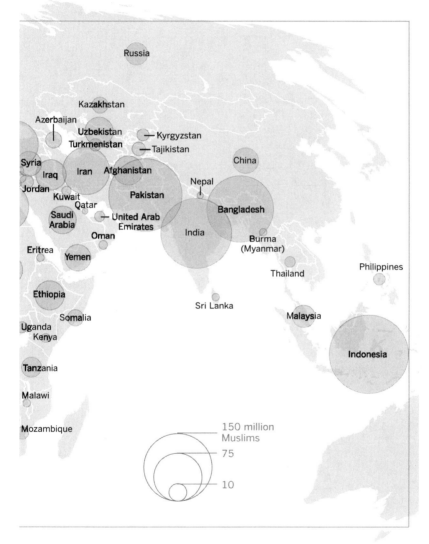

Russia

Kazakhstan

Azerbaijan

Uzbekistan — Kyrgyzstan

Turkmenistan — Tajikistan

Syria

Iraq Iran Afghanistan China

Jordan Nepal

Kuwait Pakistan

Qatar

Saudi — United Arab Bangladesh
Arabia Emirates India

Oman Burma
(Myanmar)

Eritrea

Yemen Philippines

Thailand

Ethiopia

Sri Lanka Malaysia

Somalia

Uganda
Kenya

Indonesia

Tanzania

Malawi

Mozambique

150 million
Muslims

75

10

World Distribution of Muslim Population

This 'weighted' map of the world shows each country's relative size based on its Muslim population. Figures are rounded to the nearest million.

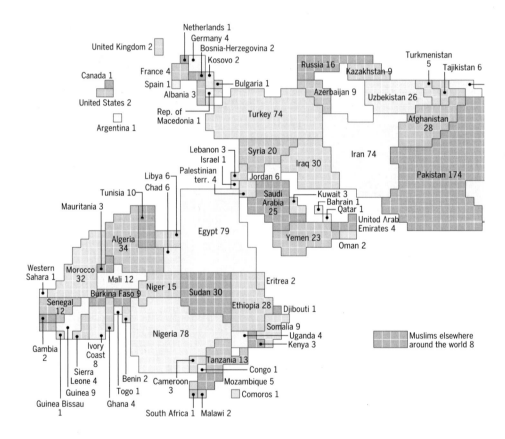

World Population 6.8 billion ⎤ **Muslim Population 1.57 billion**

· Kyrgyzstan 5

China 22

Nepal 1

India 161

Bangladesh 145

Burma (Myanmar) 2

Thailand 4

Philippines 5

Malaysia 17

Sri Lanka 2

Singapore 1

Indonesia 203

Teachers' Preface

I n a post–September 11 cultural climate, misconceptions of the Islamic faith run rampant and are perpetuated through the media, parents, and even community leaders. "Why are Muslims associated with terrorism?" has become one of the most common questions my high school students ask. Since today's high school students had only just entered school when the World Trade Center attacks took place in 2001, we cannot blame them for their misconceptions—especially given that in 2010 plans to build a mosque and Islamic center two blocks from ground zero sparked such intense anti-Muslim sentiments that the international human rights lawyer Arsalan Iftikhar, writing for CNN online, wrote about "a new wave of Islamaphobia." Without doubt, teaching about Islam can be a difficult task, but it must be done if we are to create a twenty-first-century culture of tolerance and understanding.

More than ever, we are facing a precarious task as educators. Our global economy has created new forms of instant communication and the opportunity to experience other cultures through interactive media. Our teaching model is no longer limited to text, and it is evolving as we gain access to a myriad of educational resources available through the Internet. Likewise, our students have mastered these new technologies and are often at the mercy of the constant stream of information. Students are sophisticated consumers of technology and no longer develop their beliefs through the influence of their parents and community.

Teaching Islam must be approached through several angles. First, it is imperative to teach it through a historical lens and avoid cultural bias. You will find that *This Is Islam: From Muhammad and the Community of Believers to Islam in the Global Community* offers a thorough and well-written account of the history of Islam. Encourage your students to make connections between Muhammad and other religious prophets while considering the difficulties such a revolutionary would face within their community and beyond. Primary-source sidebars, including excerpts from the Qur'an, allow students to answer their own questions through research and analysis. Of similar interest is the compelling history of hadith and the process by which this accepted canon of Muhammad's sayings and teachings was developed. Students in world religions courses might benefit from a comparison of hadith and the process by which different books were rejected or assimilated into the Christian New Testament. Both demonstrate the extent to which religious leaders shape the course of a religion into its modern counterpart. The Pillars of Faith and the Pillars of Practice form the foundation through which non-Muslims can truly understand the reason behind Islamic beliefs and practices. Misconceptions are often fueled by ignorance; therefore, students should be encouraged to develop and use their foundational knowledge of Islamic history to approach the religion's modern beliefs and practices.

As teachers of Islam, we cannot deny the impact of the faith on our students and their perceptions of Islamic culture. As one of the fastest-growing religions in the United States, Islam cannot be stereotyped as a solely Middle Eastern religion; rather, it is a religion with worldwide cultural and educational significance.

When teaching Islam, we must not avoid discussing stereotypes or misconceptions, but rather embrace the opportunity for open dialogue. It might be useful at the beginning of an Islam unit to ask your students to write down any questions they might have about the faith. This provides a secure way for students to ask questions that they would not normally ask in front of a class. This also gives you, as the educator, the ability to shape your curriculum to fit the needs of your students. Two topics that most interest students, jihad and women's legal rights, are well addressed within this book. The section on jihad, in particular, will prepare you for the inevitable questions about the connection of terrorism to Islam. Throughout the book there are informational sidebars, questions for debate, and provocative "thought experiments," all of which you can use to enrich discussion and critical thinking within your classroom. "Topics for Further Study" refer to related articles in the *Berkshire Encyclopedia of World History, 2nd Edition* (2010). Once your class's study of Islam is complete, you might ask your students to examine their previous notions about Islam and discuss ways in which they can avoid cultural and religious stereotypes. Finally, the resources in the back of the book provide further readings and websites to explore as you develop your curriculum.

When I first began teaching Islam, I struggled to find an unbiased text that comprehensively covered both Islamic history and the belief system. *This Is Islam* bridges the gap between a textbook account and a modern religions handbook by approaching the topic in a scholarly, yet approachable manner. Whether you are a first-year teacher or a veteran, I am confident that this book will be an asset to your students' study of the fascinating and complex religion Islam.

Katherine L. Saffle
Heritage Hall Upper School

This Is Islam

From Muhammad and the Community of Believers
to Islam in the Global Community

What is Islam?

slam is a religion of approximately one and a half billion people (about a quarter of the world's population). The people who profess the religion of Islam are called "Muslims" (sometimes written as "Moslems") and are found on all continents, with the largest concentrations in Asia and Africa, and to a lesser degree in Europe. Smaller populations are found in North and South America, where substantial numbers of Muslims were brought as slaves; later, the number of Muslims in the Americas increased through conversion and immigration.

"Islam" is an Arabic word meaning "submission." This term refers to the surrender of the believing Muslim to the will of God, who is seen by Muslims as all powerful and all knowing. Most Muslims believe that there is one God, who is the creator and ultimate force in the universe. All things that exist do so according to a plan designed by God and follow his laws, which conform to the laws of nature. The only things that are capable of disobeying these laws are human beings, and even they do so by God's own design. They are given the free will either to disobey or surrender voluntarily (i.e., to enter a state of Islam) to God's plan, thereby attaining salvation.

Birth of Islam

Islam's historical origins lie in the life of a man named Muhammad, who was born in Mecca (in modern-day Saudi Arabia) in either 570 or 572 CE and who died in the nearby city of Medina in 632. Islam's historical birth as a religion occurred in the early part of the seventh century CE in Mecca. Many devout Muslims would argue that, in actual fact, Islam has always existed since the religion represents God's laws for the operation of his universe, and that the historical Islam that started on the Arabian Peninsula is only the final, definitive form of Islam laid out for human understanding. This viewpoint illustrates the Muslim

1

Thought Experiment

When you think of the word "Islam," what comes to mind? What factors—such as family, politics, world events, and religion—have shaped your opinion? How do you think education, through reading a book such as *This Is Islam*, will help you and others rethink commonly held views of Islam?

---

belief in the eternal nature and validity of the religion and is not intended to contradict the historical origins of the religion.

Arabia in the Seventh Century CE

In Muhammad's time, Arabia was materially and culturally poor compared with the large and wealthy empires that surrounded it. To the north were the Byzantine Empire in Eurasia and the Sasanid dynasty in Persia, and to the south was the wealthy and vibrant Abyssinia (modern-day Ethiopia). Arabia itself was divided geographically between the main Arabian plateau and a region called South Arabia (present-day Yemen), which had once been the seat of a thriving agricultural society but had fallen on poorer times. The Arabian plateau, where Muhammad was from, was an arid place, and the majority of people lived as pastoral nomads, accompanying their herds of camels, sheep, and goats from one place to another in search of good pasture. Arabia's few cities were located on oases that provided the only reliable source of water for agriculture. Some, such as Mecca, were centers of trade for the people of Arabia and those from surrounding lands.

Modern Islam

Islam continues to be the majority religion in countries as diverse as Morocco in the west and Indonesia in the east, and from Senegal in the south to Bosnia in the north. Each country has regional expressions of Islamic practice that differ in some particulars, the most apparent being the way people dress and their customs surrounding such life events as birth and marriage. Thus, Bosnian Muslims live their lives in ways that have more in com-

---

Topics for Further Study

Islamic World

Modernity

Religion—Overview

Camels

Two children pray on prayer rugs at home. Photo by Jane Sawyer (morguefile.com).

Quick Facts: Muslims in America

In 2006, the Council on American-Islamic Relations surveyed voter-age American Muslims on their beliefs and practices. The survey uncovered the following:

* 62 percent of Muslims in the United States have at least a bachelor's degree.

* 86 percent say they celebrate the Fourth of July, and 64 percent say they fly the U.S. flag.
* 84 percent said Muslims should strongly emphasize shared values with Christians and Jews.
* 77 percent said Muslims worship the same God that Christians and Jews do.

mon with their Christian neighbors than with the Muslims of Uzbekistan or Pakistan, and the Muslims of Indonesia have incorporated many elements of Hindu mythology into their religious lives.

In other places, local customs distinguish Muslims from their non-Muslim neighbors. For example, Indian Muslims eat particular foods and do not use certain colors and flowers in their weddings in order to maintain their differences from the Hindu majority.

In spite of their differences from one part of the world to another, however, Muslims retain a remarkable similarity in their rituals, a fact that is reinforced by the almost universal use of Arabic as the language of prayer and liturgy. Furthermore, even though Muslims' sense of nationalism and patriotism is as highly developed as anyone else's, many of them retain the sense that they all belong to one community, called the *ummah*. For this reason, Muslim citizens of a particular community or country will greet fellow Muslims from distant, unrelated societies with a warmth and sense of kinship that is rare in most other religious communities.

Where Do Most Muslims Live? Are All Muslims Arabs?

Muslims can be found in virtually all countries, with most Muslims living outside the Middle East. While statistics vary, the world's largest Muslim population is found in Indonesia, followed by the Indian subcontinent. Only about 20 percent of Muslims are of Arab descent. Significant Muslim populations can be found in Central Asia, eastern Europe, and northern Africa. The Muslim population in the West has also increased significantly since the late twentieth century due to relaxed strictures on immigration and conversion (in particular, the rapid spread of Islam among African Americans).

Arabs and Arabia before Islam

he Arabs of Muhammad's time lived in tribes that were large social groups held together by a shared ancestry. Tribes were composed of a number of clans made up of several extended families. A family elder would be recognized as the leader of the clan, and the clan leaders together constituted the ruling council of a tribe. Tribal councils tried to operate through negotiation and consensus building, although powerful clans no doubt had much greater influence over tribal affairs than did weaker ones. The majority of tribes in Arabia were both patriarchal and patrilineal, meaning that not only did political and economic power reside primarily with men, but that children were regarded as the descendants of their father, but not of their mother. There appear to have been some tribes in which lineage was passed down through the mother, and even in very patriarchal tribes it was not uncommon for women to hold property. A good example is Muhammad's first wife, Khadijah, who was a wealthy widow before her marriage to Muhammad and was actively engaged in trade.

Socioeconomic Structure before Islam

Arabia had no central government or state, but existed in balance between tribes and the mercantile and agrarian cities. These cities had a close, symbiotic relationship with the nomads, who sometimes belonged to the same tribes that the town dwellers did, or else to allied tribes that came to the city to buy goods and attend religious and seasonal festivals. In return for access to the cities' markets and for employment on the trade caravans, the nomadic tribes acted as guides, provided camels, and agreed not to attack the cities or caravans on their way to or from them. Mercantile cities were heavily dependent upon the east-west trade between the Indian Ocean and the

5

This pre-Islamic coin depicts the Abyssinian king Aphidas on one side and the last Jewish king of Yemen, Yūsuf Dhū Nuwasn, on the other. Source: D. S. Margoliouth. (1905). *Mohammed and the Rise of Islam*. London: G. P. Putnam's Sons.

Mediterranean Sea, and on the north-south trade between Africa and the Byzantine Empire (c. fourth–fifteenth centuries CE) and Sasanid dynasty (224/228–651 CE). Arabia is located at the crossroads of many of the trade routes of that time, and goods were brought by ship to Arabian ports, where they were loaded onto camel caravans to be transported across the desert to distant markets.

Arabian Religion before Islam

Very little is known about the religious situation in Arabia at the time of Muhammad's birth. The surrounding empires had large Christian populations, Abyssinia and the Byzantine Empire both being Christian kingdoms. Sasanid Persia was officially Zoroastrian (a religion that sees a balance between the forces of good and evil, as distinct from Islam, Christianity, and Judaism, which are primarily organized around the recognition of one god who is viewed as entirely good). Even so, Persia had a large Christian population. In addition, all the empires had substantial Jewish populations.

There were some Christians within Arabia, but their numbers appear to have been quite small and, for the most part, they were individual believers, not entire clans or tribes who regarded themselves as Christian. No church was based within Arabia. The number of Arabian Jews appears to have been much larger; there were entirely Jewish tribes, some of which seem to have moved to Arabia from Palestine following the destruction of the temple at Jerusalem at the hands of the Romans at the end of the first century CE. It also seems probable that there were an even larger number of people who, though not formally Jews, identified themselves as Israelites and were familiar with the stories of the Hebrew prophets.

The majority of Arabs did not belong to any formal religion but believed in a combination of supernatural forces, some of which they identified as spirits and others as gods. The spirits were believed to in-

Topics for Further Study

Bands, Tribes, Chiefdoms, and States

Byzantine Empire

Caravan

A pre-Islamic inscription written in the Sabaean alphabet addresses the moon god Almaqah (c. seventh century BCE). Collection of the Louvre Museum, Paris, France.

habit natural objects, such as rocks and trees, and to have influence over human lives. The gods were often identified with natural phenomena such as the sun, moon, and rain. Of the many pre-Islamic gods, the moon god, also the guide of travelers, was viewed by many Arabs as the ancestor and leader of the others, just as Zeus was viewed by the ancient Greeks as the ancestor and chief of their gods. This did not mean that this god, named Allah (literally meaning "the God"), was the one most often worshipped; many other deities, most notably the goddesses al-Lat, al-'Uzza, and Manāt, were at the center of popular religious cults.

The pre-Islamic Arabs did not have a detailed moral and ethical code of the kind that was developed in Islamic, Christian, and Jewish theology, nor did they commonly believe in life after death. Instead, they were governed by rules of honor, courage, and hospitality. In the absence of a belief in the afterlife, the only way to attain immortality was in the memory of their tribe. People attempted to live heroic lives through extravagant acts of valor and generosity that tribal poets then rendered into verse. Poetry served as the primary form of literature in pre-Islamic Arabia, and poets were revered not only as artists but as tribal historians, because they recorded the stories of the ancestors. These Arabs were awed by the power of poetry and poets, and they viewed poets as supernaturally possessed people to be both respected and feared. A major event at most festivals of that time was a competition between poets of various tribes who would sing odes to the virtues and strengths of their own tribes and ancestors at the cost of their competitors. As such, these competitions served a role similar to that of athletic competition in modern times.

In addition to poets, two other figures carried great respect in pre-Islamic Arab society. The first was the soothsayer, who would foretell the future and

Tribal and Clan Interactions

The complex nature of tribal and clan interactions based on "honor, courage, and hospitality" formed the backbone of pre-Islamic Arabian society. One such tradition, the *gaozu* raid, functioned as a way to redistribute wealth among different tribes and clans. An important part of this raiding tradition was its emphasis on not killing members of the other tribe—taking booty was acceptable, but a death could potentially result in a blood feud and war. This tradition of raiding those more fortunate and then distributing the booty among one's own tribe has been identified as a possible religious justification for the modern Somali pirates' actions in the Indian Ocean. These modern raiders are equally focused on booty (in the form of ransoms) and trying not to kill their hostages. They see themselves as heroes, though the money usually does not make it back to their clans. Suppose this theory is correct, and the pirates see themselves as carrying on a time-honored and culturally acceptable method of raiding. How might their view make it more difficult for other societies to fight them?

attempt to solve problems as diverse as those of infertility and finding lost animals. The other was the judge, whose job it was to intercede in conflicts within a tribe and, more importantly, between tribes, as a way of avoiding violence. All these offices are significant to the study of Islam, because during Muhammad's prophetic career, he displayed qualities of all three such that his critics often labeled him as a poet or soothsayer in order to dismiss his religious claims.

Muhammad and the Emergence of Islam

Muhammad was born into the seventh-century-CE Arab environment. His family belonged to the clan of Hāshim in the tribe of Quraysh, meaning "little shark." The Quraysh was an important merchant tribe with great influence in Mecca and the surrounding area. The Hāshim clan, though not the most powerful in the tribe, was considered respectable. Mecca was home to a major shrine, called the Ka'ba, which was one of the few religious sites revered by people from all over Arabia. The Hāshim clan was the custodian of this shrine. This suggests that the Hāshim had a high degree of religious status within the tribe.

Muhammad's father, Abdallah, died shortly before Muhammad was born, and his paternal grandfather, 'Abd al-Muttalib, assumed his guardianship. When he was born, his mother, Amina, named him Ahmad, while his grandfather named him Muhammad. The latter name became more common although he is sometimes referred to as Ahmad even to this day.

Muhammad's Early Life

Little is known about Muhammad's childhood since, like other major religious figures, his life was not considered worthy of study and recording until after he became a famous prophet. The few things that we can consider to be factually true about his childhood have been embellished by pious biographers who inserted real or imagined events into his childhood in order to show that Muhammad was marked for greatness from the time of his birth. We can be reasonably sure that, in the custom among the Meccans of his day, as a very young child Muhammad was sent to the desert to live with a nomadic tribe. This custom probably derived from the desire to get children out of the unhygienic environment of the city, as well as from the belief that the nomads led a culturally "purer" (or more

Quick Facts: The Story of the Ka'ba

The Ka'ba is a cubelike structure located in the center of Masjid al-Haram, also known as the Holy Mosque or Holy House, in the pilgrimage city of Mecca. It is thought that Abraham, the founding prophet of Judaism, built the Ka'ba with his son Ishmael as a lasting monument to Allah. It contains the Black Stone, an object of veneration, which many believe fell from the heavens. In the twenty-first century, during the annual hajj, or pilgrimage season, Muslims travel from all over the world to perform rituals as a sign of devotion or worship. Participants near to the Black Stone will often kiss it, as Muhammad is thought to have done.

authentic) Arab life. Muhammad was given over to a foster family with whom he lived as a shepherd and for whom he retained a great deal of affection in later life, particularly for his foster mother, Halima. According to one popular legend, while Muhammad was herding sheep one day, he was visited by two angels, who laid him down and opened his chest. They then took out his heart and washed it in a golden basin filled with snow before replacing it and closing him up. The full implications of this story are not clear, although it probably symbolizes the removal of all existing sin from his body. There is no doubt that Muslims see in this story evidence of Muhammad's destiny to be a great prophet.

This visitation caused Muhammad's foster family to fear for his safety, and they decided to return him to his mother before something bad happened to him. Shortly after his return to Mecca, both Muhammad's mother and grandfather died, and his paternal uncle, Abu Tālib, assumed his guardianship. Abu Tālib was a merchant who frequently traveled throughout Arabia. Muhammad accompanied his uncle on these journeys, probably including one journey to Syria. In the process, he learned the merchant's trade and encountered a wide variety of people, especially Christians of different sects.

Muhammad's Marriage to Khadijah

Upon reaching adulthood, Muhammad became a merchant and quickly gained a reputation for honesty and trustworthiness. A wealthy widow named Khadijah

Bedouin Arabs are shown storytelling in this drawing by Alfred Fredericks. Source: D. S. Margoliouth. (1905). *Mohammed and the Rise of Islam*. London: G. P. Putnam's Sons.

employed him as her business representative and subsequently extended a marriage proposal to Muhammad that he accepted. At the time of their marriage, Muhammad was twenty-five years old and Khadijah was forty. In later life, Muhammad spoke fondly of the years he had spent with Khadijah, who was the mother of the only children Muhammad had who survived past infancy.

Muhammad's life with Khadijah appears to have been quiet and comfortable, although during this time he developed the habit of retiring to a cave outside Mecca to meditate in private. On one such occasion, according to the narrative record, or hadith, he fell asleep, only to be awakened by an angelic being who commanded to him, "Recite!" Muhammad replied by asking what he should recite, at which the angel only repeated his initial command. After the third time, the angel commanded, "Recite! In the name of your Lord Who created. Created man from a clot! Recite! And your Lord is Most Bountiful—He taught by the pen. Taught man that which he knew not!" (These commands became the first five lines of the Qur'an.) This event occurred when Muhammad was forty years old and marks the first revelation he received; for the remainder of his life he continued to receive revelations, sometimes through the efforts of that angelic being whom he was to identify as Gabriel, others directly from God.

Muhammad's initial reaction to his first encounter with Gabriel was to run home to seek comfort from Khadijah. Over time, she persuaded him to listen to the angel, and Muhammad was convinced that he had been chosen as a prophet of God to bring a divine message to humankind. The major parts of this message were the existence of a unique, all-powerful God, a warning of an impending doomsday and judgment, and an encouragement to live a virtuous life.

Great Emigration: The Hijra

At first Muhammad's preaching was met with tolerance and curiosity, but as he started to gain converts, the leaders of Mecca began to view him as a threat and to persecute his followers. The majority of Muhammad's early followers are believed to have been women, slaves, and the very poor, all of whom were at the mercy of their powerful oppressors. When it became clear to Muhammad that it would be impossible for his followers and him to live in Mecca in peace, he began to search for a new place to live. It so happened that a nearby town, Yathrib (modern-day Medina), was politically divided between two powerful tribes, and they were looking for an impartial judge to arbitrate between them. Muhammad's reputation as an honest man reached that city, and the elders of Yathrib invited him to move there and serve as their judge. Muhammad agreed to do so only if certain conditions were fulfilled: (1) that his family and followers

Thought Experiment

Imagine that the year is 615 CE and you live in a bustling trade city in Saudi Arabia that is home to a diverse population of Greeks, Jews, Egyptians, Africans, and Arabs. Your society mostly worships multiple gods at a local temple that contains a black stone. One day while at the market, you hear of a man proclaiming that he is the messenger of God and that there is only one God. Many people think he is a sorcerer and that his divine visions are hallucinations. Others see him as a threat because his message of social justice would upset the hierarchical structure of your society. What measures could you and others take to decide whether he speaks the truth? What would it ultimately take for people to believe his message?

could move with him; (2) that they would be supported until they could find a means of livelihood for themselves; and (3) that they would be considered full citizens of the city in such a way that, if the Meccans and their allies chose to attack the Muslims, then all the citizens of Yathrib would fight on the side of Muhammad's followers, called the "Muslims."

The delegation from Yathrib agreed to these terms, and the Muslims' secret migration from Mecca to that city began. Finally, when all but two of Muhammad's followers (his friend and adviser, Abū Bakr, and his cousin 'Alī) had reached Yathrib, he decided to move there himself. By this time, some of his opponents had realized that he represented a grave threat to their interests and had formed a pact to kill him. Hearing of their plan, Muhammad secretly left Mecca accompanied by Abū Bakr, leaving 'Alī in his house. 'Alī was the son of Muhammad's uncle Abu Tālib and had come to live with Muhammad as his adopted son. 'Alī eventually married Muhammad's daughter Fātimah and became one of the most important and influential people in the formative period of Islam.

That night Muhammad's enemies surrounded his house, waiting to attack him in the dark. 'Alī served as a decoy by sleeping in Muhammad's bed. When the Meccans finally broke into Muhammad's house and found 'Alī, they realized that Muhammad had slipped away, and they sent a search party to hunt him down. Legend has it that Muhammad and Abū Bakr hid in a cave to escape their pursuers and that a spider wove a web covering the entrance to the cave. Seeing the spiderweb, the Meccans thought that no one had been inside in a while and did not enter the cave in search of Muhammad. After the search party had returned empty handed, Muhammad and Abū Bakr made their way to Yathrib, and 'Alī followed as soon as he had settled all of Muhammad's financial and social obligations in Mecca.

The emigration of Muhammad and the Muslims from Mecca to Yathrib, which occurred in 622 CE, marks the most important date in Islamic history. It is called the Hijrah, or "Great Emigration." The Muslims who emigrated are referred to as "Muhajirs," and those who helped them as "Ansar." Great honor is attached to both groups. Throughout Islamic history, any event in which a number of Muslims have to flee from persecution to a safe haven is seen as a reference to the Hijra, and the émigrés and their helpers are seen as repeating the events in

Topics for Further Study

Muhammad

Pastoral Nomadic Societies

Trading Patterns, Trans-Saharan

Muhammad's life. The Hijra is also important because it marks the start of the Islamic calendar, which is used for all religious events and is the official calendar in many countries to this day.

The Hijra marks the beginning of Islam as a social religion and political entity. In Mecca, Muhammad was viewed mostly as someone who issued warnings and as a prophet who brought a message of monotheism, urging people to repent of their immoral ways before it was too late. In Yathrib, the religion began to evolve into a social phenomenon and developed a history and complex set of laws. The importance of Yathrib in the development of Islam is attested to by the fact that the city was renamed Madinat al-Nabi ("City of the Prophet"), Medina or al-Madīnah, for short. While at Medina, the revelations that Muhammad received began to emphasize social laws and a sense of history that showed Muhammad and his religion to be a continuation of the religious tradition of the Hebrew prophets. Muhammad rapidly rose from the status of a simple prophet to that of the social, religious, and political leader of an entire community. As such, he resembled religious figures such as Moses, David, and Solomon much more than he resembled Jesus or the Buddha.

The Meccans perceived the growing Muslim community of Medina as a threat and engaged in three battles with them. Each battle resulted in Muhammad's cause becoming much stronger, so that within a decade he had become the most powerful figure in all of Arabia. Finally, in 630 CE, the city of Mecca surrendered to Muhammad and he entered it, guaranteeing the citizens security of their lives and property. Even the leaders of Mecca were untouched. The only major consequences were the executions of poets and singers who had ridiculed Muhammad and his religion and carried out a concerted propaganda campaign against him, and the removal of all idols from the Ka'ba. Muhammad then performed a pilgrimage to the Ka'ba and returned to Medina, which he now considered his home. He made one more journey to Mecca before his death in order to visit the Ka'ba. This is called the "Farewell Pilgrimage" and serves as the model for one of the most important Islamic rituals.

Shortly after his return from the Farewell Pilgrimage, Muhammad fell gravely ill and confined himself to the house of his third wife 'Ā'ishah, who was the daughter of Abū Bakr, where he died on 8 June 632. According to a tradition stating that prophets should be buried where they die, Muhammad was buried in 'Ā'ishah's chamber. It was later converted into a shrine and serves as an important pilgrimage site to this day.

The Ka'ba, thought to be built by Abraham and Ishmael, is a focal point of Islamic faith.
Source: D. S. Margoliouth. (1905). *Mohammed and the Rise of Islam*. London: G. P. Putnam's Sons.

The *Ummah* after Muhammad

Muhammad died without appointing a definite successor. Although it was clear that there would be no prophets after him, no one was sure what the role of the leader after him was to be. The elders of the *ummah* decided that Muhammad's closest companion, Abū Bakr, who was also one of the first converts to Islam, should lead the community after his death. Abū Bakr died in 634 CE, two years after Muhammad and was succeeded by another respected companion of Muhammad named 'Umar (c. 586–644 CE). It was during 'Umar's ten-year leadership and the twelve years of his successor, 'Uthmān ibn 'Affān (d. 656 CE), that the Islamic community burst out of Arabia and spread from the Mediterranean shores of North Africa to the Central Asian steppe. It was also during their time that the revelations received by Muhammad were organized into a scripture called the Qur'an (or Koran).

The leaders of the *ummah* after Muhammad were neither prophets nor kings. Instead, they were known as caliphs (*khalīfa* in Arabic), a word that means "representative" or "delegate," implying that the caliphs did not rule on their own authority but only as the representative successors of God and the Prophet Muhammad in terms of leadership of the polity. After 'Uthmān ibn 'Affān's death there was some confusion as to who should be the next caliph. Many people felt that the honor should go to Muhammad's cousin and son-in-law, 'Alī (also known as 'Alī ibn Abī Tālib; c. 600–661 CE). Others supported 'Uthmān ibn 'Affān's cousin Mu'āwiyah. Encouraged by their respective supporters, both men were declared caliphs and a civil war ensued. In the course of the dispute, 'Alī was murdered by an assassin and Mu'āwiyah successfully seized power for himself and his family. This laid the foundations for the first Islamic dynasty, which was known as the Umayyad (a reference

'Ā'ishah (614–678 CE)

'Ā'ishah was the daughter of Muhammad's close companion and first caliph, Abū Bakr. She was very young when Muhammad married her and was his only wife who was not previously married (his other wives were either widows or divorcées). Given her assertive personality and high status as the daughter of Muhammad's most senior companion, 'Ā'ishah had the most impact of any of Muhammad's wives on determining the course of Islamic history and religion. She outlived Muhammad by almost fifty years and was considered a very reliable source of information about him. As such, she had tremendous influence on the formation of the hadith (religious narrative) and Islamic law. Furthermore, she never hesitated to get involved in the political life of the *ummah* (community). She publicly disagreed with 'Umar even after he became the second caliph, and she was so opposed to 'Alī becoming caliph that she and a group of her followers went to war against him in 656 CE.

Despite being a constant source of trouble for them, both 'Alī and 'Umar treated her with immense respect because of the great affection that Muhammad had for her. When Muhammad fell prey to the illness that eventually took his life, he moved into 'Ā'ishah's room. He died there and, in keeping with a tradition that states that prophets should be buried where they die, he was buried there. 'Ā'ishah refused to move out of her chamber (now essentially a tomb) and lived there until the end of her life.

to Mu'āwiyah's clan). The majority of modern pious Muslims believe that with the rise of the Umayyad dynasty, the pristine institution of the caliphate came to an end; they only consider the first four caliphs as truly virtuous; as a result, those four are referred to as the Rightly Guided Caliphs. Even so, it was under the hundred-year rule of the Umayyads that most of the lands still identified with Islam were conquered, and the Islamic Empire extended from modern-day Spain to Pakistan.

Even though the Umayyads were in almost complete political control, the dispute between the supporters of 'Alī's descendants and the Umayyads did not end. It took an even more serious turn when 'Alī's son Husayn and many of his family members were massacred in 680 CE by troops loyal to Mu'āwiyah's son, Yazīd, at a place in modern-day Iraq called Karbala. This formed the basis of a split within the Islamic community that continues to this day with the separation between the Sunni and Shi'a sects.

Many pious Muslims of that time were disillusioned by the political conflict raging around them and withdrew into a pious contemplation of their faith. Some emphasized the role of prayer and love for God, others devoted themselves to preaching among the citizens of the newly conquered lands, while still others dedicated their lives to the study of the Qur'an and traditions of Muhammad and his companions. It was primarily through the efforts of such people that the worldwide Islamic community developed a rich and vibrant tradition for theology, law, and philosophy and that the citizens of very diverse lands converted to the new religion.

One of the most remarkable features of Islam is that, with only one significant exception, all lands to which it spread have remained Muslim into modern times. The exception is Spain, where the long process of Christian reconquest (called the Reconquista) followed by the Spanish Inquisition systematically eradicated the Muslim population of Spain after 1492. Even so, when the edict

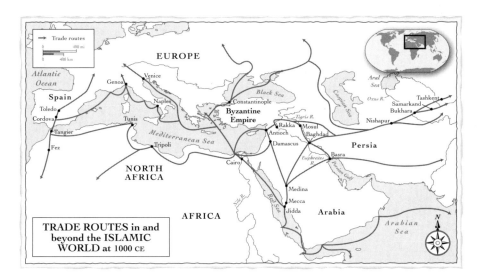

for the final expulsion of Muslims and Jews was issued in 1619 (127 years after the end of the Reconquista), approximately 2 million Muslims fled the kingdom of Castille alone. This gives some indication of the degree to which Islam had been integrated into Spanish life.

Islamic Texts

Islam is a religion with many texts, and the tradition views scripture (defined as a divinely revealed text) as the greatest evidence of God's involvement in human life. Islam's followers have developed a number of sciences to study this scripture as well as a number of art forms to celebrate it. Although the Qur'an is Islam's only scripture, there are other writings that Muslims consider to carry great religious importance. Despite their inferior status to the Qur'an, these texts can be viewed as scriptural as well, since they are often quoted as sources of religious authority and are used to derive religious law.

The Qur'an

The word "Qur'an" derives from the Arabic verb meaning "to read" or "to recite." Qur'an therefore means something like a recitation or a collection of things to be recited. Muslims seldom refer to their scripture simply as the Qur'an but normally add a title that signifies respect, such as al-Karim ("the Noble") or al-'Azim ("the Magnificent"). Within the Qur'an itself, the term al-Kitab ("the Book") is used as an alternative.

In Muhammad's opinion, and that of the majority of pious believers, the Qur'anic revelations came from heaven, where they were preserved on a "well-guarded tablet," a concealed supernatural book that existed in the presence of God. Muhammad did not become acquainted with the whole of the Qur'an at once but only with isolated sections of it. The Qur'an contains only a few obscure hints about how it was communicated to Muhammad. In fact, it is not from the Qur'an but from the traditions of Muhammad's life (called "hadith") that we learn about the trances Muhammad occasionally went into when he received a revelation. On such occasions, he would begin to tremble and ask to be covered up with a cloak. He would then hear a revelation and recite it to those around him, or in formal situations, to larger gatherings.

19

Quick Facts: Why Is Arabic So Important to Islam?

The primary scripture of Islam, the Qur'an, is considered to be the direct, word-for-word revelation of God. Since it is in Arabic, Muslims continue to read and recite it in the Arabic language regardless of their mother tongue. Therefore, although most Muslims are not of Arab origin, many learn to read and write Arabic at an early age, just as Jews traditionally learn Hebrew. Arabic is to Islam as Latin was to Christianity, and since Islamic scholarship was overwhelmingly conducted in Arabic, a familiarity with Arabic also allows Muslims to engage the centuries of scholastic dialogue and literary heritage. Many times, Muslim pilgrims to the holy city of Mecca find that they can communicate with some of their fellow pilgrims from around the world through a rudimentary understanding of Arabic. Due to the influence of Arabic, many languages spoken in Islamic lands have adopted Arabic words, such as the universally understood greeting *salaam 'alaykum* or "peace be upon you," or words for the ritual practices and ethical ideals of Islam, such as *salah* for "ritual prayers" and *akhlaq* for "good morality." Some Islamic concepts, such as sharia (Islamic ritual law and legal injunctions), do not always translate easily and thus have been retained in Arabic throughout the Muslim world, while others, such as the *hijab* ("the veil") are often retained in lieu of modern translations with negative connotations.

Muhammad believed that not only his prophetic mission but also the revelations of the earlier Hebrew prophets and the holy scriptures of the Jews and Christians were based on the original heavenly scripture, so that they coincided in part with what he himself taught. The Qur'an thus confirms what was revealed earlier: the law was given to Moses in the Torah, to Jesus as recorded in the Gospels, and, in less famous revealed texts, to other prophets included in the Hebrew Bible.

Although the stories contained in the Qur'an and the concept of revelation through a series of prophets are shared with the Hebrew Bible and the New

Jabal-al-Noor, or Mountain of Light, is where Muhammad is said to have prayed and meditated.

Testament, the style of the Qur'an is more in keeping with that of the pre-Islamic Arab religious tradition of soothsayers. The text is neither written in prose nor is it poetry, but consists of rhymed prose that is easier to remember than normal prose but is not as restricted in style as poetry.

Organizing the Qur'an

The Qur'an is arranged into 114 chapters, or *suras*. The *suras* are of unequal length, some being several pages long while others are only a few lines. Their

Worth Debating

What purpose does a holy text serve for a religious group? What value might a religious text be to either people of other faiths or to nonbelievers?

order does not reflect the order of revelation; instead they are arranged by length, from longest to shortest, with the exception of the first *sura*, "The Opening," which has seven verses. *Suras* are traditionally identified by their names rather than their numbers. Their names are normally distinctive or unusual words that appear somewhere in the early part of the *sura*. They are further subdivided into verses called *ayat* (literally "signs"). Twenty-nine of the *suras* begin with seemingly disjointed letters referred to as the "mysterious letters." The most common religious interpretation for their existence is that they are an integral part of the text and carry some secret religious meaning. Many other explanations for them exist, however, including one that suggests that they were part of a filing system used to organize *suras* into the Qur'an.

Collecting the Qur'an

The Qur'an was not compiled during Muhammad's lifetime but was preserved on whatever material was then available: bits of parchment, leaves, shoulder blades of camels, and especially in the oral tradition, memorized in sequence by his followers. After Muhammad's death, people decided to start collecting the work, but the process took several years. There is a popular story that asserts that the Qur'an was collected in its present form while Abū Bakr was caliph. According to this account, 'Umar was disturbed by the fact that in one of the early battles under Abū Bakr, many of the people who knew the Qur'an by heart were killed. 'Umar feared that if more of them died, some of the Qur'an would be lost forever. He therefore counseled Abū Bakr to make a collection of the Qur'an. At first, Abū Bakr hesitated to undertake a task

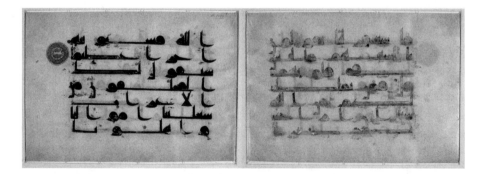

The *sura* on this fragment is written in *Kufic* script and follows the format typical of horizontal Qur'ans written on parchment in the ninth century CE. Library of Congress.

that the Prophet hadn't authorized before his death, but in the end he agreed and commissioned one of Muhammad's secretaries, named Zayd ibn Thābit (c. seventh century CE), to direct the project. According to this account of how the Qur'an was collected, Zayd wrote what he had transcribed the parts onto sheets of equal size and gave this "book" to Abū Bakr. On the latter's death, the book was passed to 'Umar and then to his daughter Hafsah, a widow of Muhammad. This collection then served as the model from which all later copies of the Qur'an were made.

This story may not be true. It assumes that during Muhammad's lifetime no one attempted to make an authoritative record of the revelations. There is also much disagreement about who first came up with the idea of collecting the Qur'an. Generally, it is said to be 'Umar, but sometimes Abū Bakr is said to have commissioned the collection on his own. On the other hand, there is a tradition that says 'Umar was the first to collect the Qur'an and it completely excludes Abū Bakr. The greatest criticism of this theory is that a collection put together under the authority of someone such as Abū Bakr with the help of 'Umar and Zayd ibn Thābit would have had a tremendous amount of importance and authority, but this does not appear to have been the case. Several different collections were considered authoritative in various provinces of the Islamic world. Furthermore, the disputes over the accurate text of the Qur'an that arose while 'Uthmān ibn 'Affān was caliph, and that eventually led to the official codification of the Qur'an, would not have arisen had there been an official version in the possession of the caliph. Thus it appears that no official collection of the Qur'an was made while Abū Bakr was caliph.

Under the caliph 'Uthmān ibn 'Affān, there were disputes concerning which version was the official version of the Qur'an. During military campaigns in the Caucasus, arguments arose between troops drawn from Syria and Iraq over the exact text of some verses of the Qur'an. This disagreement rose to such a level that a general had to bring the problem to the attention of the caliph. 'Uthmān ibn 'Affān took counsel with other senior companions of the Prophet and finally order Zayd ibn Thābit to collect the Qur'an. Zayd ibn Thābit, assisted by three highly respected assistants, collected fragments of revelation from a variety of sources. The

Topics for Further Study

Arab Caliphates

Culture

Deserts

History, Oral

whole Qur'an was then carefully organized and compared with the private copy in the possession of 'Umar's daughter, Hafsah. Finally, an authoritative text of the Qur'an was established. A number of copies were made and distributed to the main Islamic centers. Previously existing copies were said to have been destroyed, so that the text of all subsequent copies of the Qur'an would be based upon that standard edition. This establishment of the text of the Qur'an under 'Uthmān ibn 'Affān may be dated somewhere between 650 and 656 CE, and is a critical point in what may be called the formation of the canon of the Qur'an. Whatever may have been the previous form of the Qur'an, it is almost certain that the modern version is essentially the Qur'an of 'Uthmān ibn 'Affān's time. His commission decided what was to be included and excluded; it also fixed the number and order of the *suras*.

While 'Uthmān ibn 'Affān's efforts to make the official version of the Qur'an the only one for the entire *ummah* were largely successful, unofficial versions of the Qur'an were not forgotten. Most early histories and commentaries on the Qur'an mention a number of other collections; some have lists explaining how they differed from 'Uthmān ibn 'Affān's edition. The information suggests there was no great variation in the actual contents of the Qur'an in the period immediately after the Prophet's death. Differences consisted mostly of minor problems arising because the order of the *suras* was apparently not fixed, and there were also slight variations in some of the words.

While the promulgation of the official text of the Qur'an under 'Uthmān ibn 'Affān was a major step toward uniformity in versions of the scripture, its importance may easily be exaggerated. For one thing, knowledge of the Qur'an among Muslims was based far more on memory than on writing. For another, the early Arabic script of the Qur'an was a sort of shorthand: only consonants were written, and the same letter shape could indicate more than one sound. This script was simply an aid to memorization; it assumed that the reader had some familiarity with the text. It was not until the reign of the Umayyad caliph 'Abd al-Malik ibn Marwān (served 685–705 CE) that the modern Arabic script was created with its vowels and the use of one letter shape for each sound.

Hadith

Although Muslims treat the Qur'an as the only formal scripture of their religion, other written religious works of great importance to Islam exist. Sunnis, in particular, rely heavily on a category of literature called hadith. The word "hadith" primarily means "a communication" or "a narrative." In Islamic terms, it means a record of the actions or sayings of the Prophet and his companions. In the latter sense, the whole body of the sacred tradition of Islam is called the hadith and the formal study of it is called the science of hadith.

Pre-Islamic Arabs considered it a virtue to follow the example or tradition of their forefathers. But in the Islamic period, a person could hardly follow the example of ancestors who were not Muslim, so a new tradition of practices, or *sunna*, had to be found: the *sunna* of Muhammad. At first companions of Muhammad were considered the best sources for his *sunna*: they had listened to the Prophet and witnessed his actions with their own eyes. The term "companion" eventually came to be a technical term connoting any Muslim who was alive at Muhammad's time and could possibly have seen him on even one occasion. The generation immediately after them became known as "the followers," and those after them "the followers of the followers."

After Muhammad's death, the original religious ideas and usages that had prevailed in the *ummah* could not remain unaltered for long. A new period of development set in. The learned systematically began to develop the doctrine of duties and beliefs in accordance with the new conditions prevailing in the Islamic community. After the early conquests under the Umayyads, Islam was practiced in an enormous area, and new ideas and institutions were brought in with the conquered peoples. Nevertheless, the principle was steadfastly adhered to that only the *sunna* of the Prophet and that of the original Muslim community could supply rules of conduct for the Muslim believers. This soon led to deliberate forgery of traditions concerning the Prophet. Transmitters of hadith traditions brought the words and actions of the Prophet into agreement with their own views and ideals.

Numerous traditions were thus put into circulation alleging that Muhammad said or did something that would support a particular opinion. A very large portion of these sayings ascribed to Muhammad dealt with legal provisions, religious obligations, issues of what was permissible and forbidden, ritual purity, and matters of etiquette and courtesy. Over time the records of Muhammad's words and deeds increased in quantity and copiousness. In the early centuries after Muhammad's death, there was great

Topics for Further Study

Islam

Kinship

Writing Systems and Materials

diversity of opinion in the Muslim community on many questions relating to topics such as those mentioned above. Each party tried to support its views as far as possible with sayings and decisions of the Prophet. The conditions became so bad that an entire category of prophetic traditions made up of sayings ascribed to Muhammad arose to deal with places and lands that were not conquered until after he had died.

Hadith as History

The majority of hadith accounts cannot be regarded as reliable historical accounts of the *sunna* of the Prophet. On the contrary, they express opinions that had come to be held in different circles in the early centuries after Muhammad's death and were only then ascribed to the Prophet. The hadith, however, is held in great reverence throughout Islamic society. In some cases, it is even believed that God's actual words are found in the hadith. Such accounts usually begin with the words "God said" and are called "Divine Hadith" (Hadith Qudsi). It is not completely clear how they originally differed from the material that was included in the Qur'an. But few modern Muslims would confuse a Qur'anic verse with a "Divine Hadith."

As early as the eighth century CE, certain Islamic scholars became extremely concerned about the large number of forged hadith that were in circulation, and they devised a highly elaborate system to establish some idea of a hadith's accuracy. According to the Muslim view, a hadith account can only be considered believable if its chain of transmission, or *isnad*, offers an unbroken series of reliable authorities. The critical examination of an *isnad* consisted of research into the names and circumstances of the transmitters in a hadith account in order to investigate when and where they lived and which of them had been personally acquainted with one another, and a test their reliability, truthfulness, and accuracy in transmitting the texts, to make certain which of the hadith transmitters were reliable. Scholars used the chain of transmitters to divide a hadith into three main categories that denote their reliability. The most important of these are called *sahih* (sound). This name is given to those hadith considered absolutely reliable because they have flawless chains of transmission and reinforce something that is widely accepted in the Islamic community. The next class of traditions, those considered reliable but not without doubt about their authenticity, are called *hasan* (beautiful). Finally, some hadith were judged to be unreliable or "weak."

Thought Experiment

Some people compare the validity of the different categories of the narrative record, or hadith, to the game of telephone, where a person whispers a statement to another person, who whispers it to another person, and so on. The final statement is different from the original. Try passing on particular verses from the hadith to your classmates, starting at on one end of the classroom and finishing at the other. Listen to the resulting verse at the end. Oral tradition often changes the meaning of sayings over time. How does this exercise demonstrate oral tradition in action?

Hadith Collections

Many collections of hadith traditions were prepared by scholars in the eighth and ninth centuries CE. At first, the hadith accounts in these collections were arranged according to their transmitters rather than their content. The best known of these is by an important and respected religious scholar named Ahmad ibn Hanbal (780–855 CE). But arrangement according to transmitters made the collections difficult to use when looking for hadith by topic, which is the way hadith are most often used. Later collections were therefore arranged in chapters dealing with specific topics. Six such hadith collections became extremely popular in the Islamic culture, of which two, one by a scholar named Muslim ibn al-Hajjāj (c. 817–875 CE) and the other by al-Bukhārī (810–870), are considered so reliable many Sunni Muslims rank them just below the Qur'an as sacred texts. Al-Bukhārī and Muslim ibn al-Hajjāj's books only contain those hadith accounts they judged to be *sahih*, or completely above any suspicion regarding their accuracy. Shi'a Muslims do not rely on hadith literature in the same way as do Sunnis, but they too, have their own collections of hadith that they consider important.

Sunna (Tradition of Muhammad)

What is contained in the hadith is the *sunna*, or tradition, of Muhammad, consisting of his actions and sayings and those things to which he gave unspoken approval. *Sunna* has come to mean the practice of the greater *ummah*, and in this capacity it is often referred to as the "Living Sunna." Muhammad's *sunna*, in the sense of his actions and words, is contained in the hadith. In theory, the concepts of *sunna* and hadith are separate, but in practice they often coincide.

To understand the importance of the *sunna* in Islam, we must remember that while the Qur'an was a source from which a major part of Islamic practice was derived, Muhammad had settled many questions posed to him not by revelation but by decisions made on a case by case basis. His words and actions were recognized—even in his own lifetime—as a fine example deserving to be imitated. This is why the *sunna* of the Prophet was fixed in writing, although it never gained an importance equal to that of the Qur'an.

It is clear, however, that the *sunna* became a standard of behavior alongside the Qur'an, and that religious scholars tried to answer questions concerning the relationship between the two. In the earliest Islamic community, the *sunna* appears to have been equal to the Qur'an in authority. With the passage of time and the conversion of non-Arab peoples to Islam, the Qur'an gained a centrality as scripture that outstripped the importance given to the *sunna*, particularly in its written form of hadith.

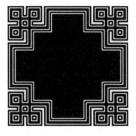

Islamic Sects

*T*he Islamic community is divided into a number of sects, the most important of which derive their differences from events that occurred in the first two centuries of Islamic history. Over the centuries, several other sects emerged; some, such as the Nurbakhshia, a small, mystical sect limited to a remote region of the western Himalayas, are too small to have exerted much influence over the *ummah* at large. Others, such as the Wahhabiya, which is an eighteenth-century reform movement within the major Islamic sect of Sunnism, became powerful enough to take over in some countries (Saudi Arabia, in this case) and have considerable influence in the greater Islamic society. Still others, such as the Bahá'í faith, were perceived by others and by their own practitioners to be so different from the Islamic environment in which they emerged that they no longer consider themselves Muslims and have emerged as independent religions. Nevertheless, these later sectarian movements all occur within a context where the Muslim community is essentially divided in two unequal parts, the Sunni majority and a number of smaller sects that together make up the Shi'a minority.

Sunnism

Sunnis account for the overwhelming majority of all Muslims. The term "Sunni" derives from the word *sunna* ("tradition") and is actually an abbreviation for a much longer term meaning "the people of tradition and the community." This name was applied to those members of the early *ummah* who were political quietists, believing that it was better to accept a less-than-ideal leader than to risk the destruction of the Muslim community through civil war.

Given the meaning of Sunni, the only way for an individual to separate from Sunnism is to consciously take up a political or religious position that opposes the conventional views of the Sunni majority. At most times in history, the Sunni sect has taken an inclusive attitude and tried to count as many Muslims as it could within the Sunni umbrella, even when it meant that notions of what was acceptable as Sunni belief had to be expanded. It is important to note that being a Sunni does not necessarily imply that an individual agrees with the way the Sunni Muslim community is being governed; it simply means that it is more important to maintain a safe Muslim community than to fight a bad ruler.

A major difference between Sunnism and Shi'ism is that, unlike Shi'ism, Sunnism has no official notion of a clergy or other kind of formal religious leadership. Sunni religious scholars gain authority through their reputations for learning and high moral character, not through a system of ordination (though the system in Shi'ism is also more informal than in Christianity). In the classical age of Islam (c. seventh century CE), this allowed for a high degree of diversity in the opinions of scholars and permitted a large class of people to engage in *ijtihad*, or the practice of independent reasoning, in thinking about Islamic law and theology.

In practice, in many parts of the Sunni Muslim community since the sixteenth century CE, religious scholars have been employees of the state and have been extremely sensitive to the wishes of their rulers in making controversial statements. They have also adopted distinctive forms of dress to show their status as religious scholars. As such, Sunnism has developed a clerical system in which religious scholars go to different colleges than other people and are immediately recognized by the clothing they wear.

Shi'ism

The word "Shi'a" literally means "party" or "faction," which gives a clear indication that the early Shi'a believers (sometimes called "Shi'ite believers") saw themselves as a political, rather than a purely religious, group. They were referred to as the "Shi'at 'Ali" ("the Party of 'Ali," Muhammad's cousin and son-in-law), and were some of 'Ali's closest friends. The original Shi'a followers believed that 'Ali should have been recognized as the leader of the *ummah* after Muhammad's death, and that after 'Ali, this leadership should have been kept within the household of the Prophet. This belief is supported by many hadith traditions in which Muhammad is believed to have shown a preference for his family over other members of his community, and by other traditions according to which, in his absence, he used to designate 'Ali as the temporary leader of the Islamic community.

Despite the belief by some members of the early Muslim community that 'Ali be made leader, he was passed over in favor of three of Muhammad's close companions. When he did finally become leader of the *ummah*, his brief

Quick Facts: Sunni and Shi'a Muslims

In the twenty-first century, Sunni Muslims outnumber Shi'a Muslims nearly 7 to 1. The development of these two sects over time has created theological and religious tensions between them that affect political, diplomatic, and social conditions in the modern Islamic world. Powerful Islamic dynasties in the sixteenth and seventeenth centuries firmly established Sunni Islam throughout the Middle East and in Turkey (center of the Ottoman Empire, c. 1300–1922), and they established Shi'a Islam in Iran and Iraq (center of the Safavid Empire, 1501–1722). During this time, the Sunnis persecuted Shi'a Muslims, who in turn persecuted Sunnis in their respective lands. Although this violent animosity subsided somewhat in the nineteenth century, modern times have seen a resurgence, especially in Iraq under the Baath Party after 1968. This Sunni ruling party (in a country that is 60 percent Shi'a Muslim) rooted out political and religious opposition by conducting mass killings through military might. In recent years, mass graves have been discovered that reveal the brutality of the regime of former Iraqi president Saddam Hussein, which resulted in the deaths of tens of thousands of Iraqi Shi'a Muslims.

Meanwhile, neighboring Iran, with a population that is nearly 100 percent Shi'a Muslim, has generally isolated itself from the rest of the Islamic world. It also adopted an extreme interpretation of many aspects of Islam, including restrictions on the public role of women and, in particular, approaches to jihad and relations with non-Muslims. After the Iranian Revolution of 1979, the theocratic government led by Ayatollah Khomeini launched a jihad against Iraq and took a more isolationist and aggressive posture toward the rest of the world. This position continues into the twenty-first century, even though new personalities have assumed leadership in both the religious and political hierarchies in Iran.

five-year reign was plagued with political problems. Following the assassination of 'Alī in 661 CE, political control passed to his rival Mu'āwiyah and eventually to the Umayyad dynasty. Throughout this period, however, the supporters of 'Alī did not stop believing in the legitimacy of their claim and engaged in ongoing political agitation.

The conflict between the Shi'a sect and the supporters of Mu'āwiyah reached a crisis point in 680 CE with the murder of 'Alī's son, Husayn, together with many members of his family. After this event, the Shi'a community was not able to wield much political power for quite some time, and consequently spent less time emphasizing the political dimension of Shi'ism and more time developing distinctive and elaborate theological ideas concerning the nature of Shi'ism. But the political experiences of the early Shi'a community had a direct bearing on Shi'ite beliefs, which emphasize the importance of martyrdom and persecution.

Shi'a Imams

There are three main branches of Shi'a Islam, all of which are united by a common belief that the only legitimate leader of the Muslim community is a descendant of

Calligrapher Husayn Zarrin Qalam's eighteenth-century calligraphic panel uses *nasta 'līq* **script for the letters of the larger words, which are filled in with decorative motifs, animals, and human figures in a style called** *gulzar* **(meaning "rose garden" or "full of flowers"). Surrounding the larger,** *nasta 'līq* **letters are small Shi'a prayers executed in a variety of scripts.** Library of Congress.

'Alī and his wife Fātima, the daughter of the Prophet. This leader, known as the "imam," is considered superior to other human beings because of his bloodline and is chosen by God to lead the Muslim community. The three main Shi'a sects agree on the identities of the first four imams. They disagree over the fifth, with the majority believing that Husayn's grandson, Muhammad al-Baqir (d. 731 CE) was the rightful imam, and the minority following al-Baqir's brother, Zayd (d. 740 CE), resulting in their being called Zaydis.

Selected Sayings of 'Alī ibn Abī Tālib

The speeches, letters, and sayings of 'Alī ibn Abī Tālib, the first imam according to Shi'a Muslims, were collected into the *Nahj al-Balaghah*. A selection of his sayings follows:

1. He who is greedy is disgraced; he who discloses his hardship will always be humiliated; he who has no control over his tongue will often have to face discomfort.

2. Avarice is disgrace; cowardice is a defect; poverty often disables an intelligent man from arguing his case; a poor man is a stranger in his own town; misfortune and helplessness are calamities; patience is a kind of bravery; to sever attachments with the wicked world is the greatest wealth; piety is the best weapon of defence.

3. Submission to Allah's will is the best companion; wisdom is the noblest heritage; theoretical and practical knowledge are the best signs of distinction; deep thinking will present the clearest picture of every problem.

4. The mind of a wise man is the safest custody of secrets; cheerfulness is the key to friendship; patience and forbearance will conceal many defects.

5. A conceited and self-admiring person is disliked by others; charity and alms are the best remedy for ailments and calamities; one has to account in the next world for the deeds that he has done in this world.

6. Live amongst people in such a manner that if you die they weep over you and if you are alive they crave for your company.

7. If you overpower your enemy, then pardon him by way of thankfulness to Allah, for being able to subdue him.

8. Unfortunate is he who cannot gain a few sincere friends during his life and more unfortunate is the one who has gained them and then lost them (through his deeds).

9. When some blessings come to you, do not drive them away through thanklessness.

10. He who is deserted by friends and relatives will often find help and sympathy from strangers.

11. Every person who is tempted to go astray does not deserve punishment.

12. One who rushes madly after inordinate desire runs the risk of encountering destruction and death.

13. Overlook and forgive the weaknesses of the generous people because if they fall down, Allah will help them.

14. Failures are often the results of timidity and fears; disappointments are the results of bashfulness; hours of leisure pass away like summer clouds, therefore, do not waste opportunity of doing good.

15. If someone's deeds lower his position, his pedigree cannot elevate it.

Zaydis

Zayd was the first person since the massacre of Husayn and his family at Karbala in 680 CE to try to wrest political power from the Umayyads by force. After spending a year in preparation in the heavily fortified Shi'a city of al-Kufa in Iraq, he came out with a group of followers but was killed in battle.

Zaydi beliefs are similar to those of the major Shi'a sect, that of the Twelvers. The main difference is in the Zaydi ideas concerning the imam. They believe that any descendant of 'Alī and Fātima can be the imam, regardless of whether they are descended from Husayn or his elder brother Hasan. In order to be acknowledged as the imam, a person must have the ability to resort to the sword if necessary. For this reason, no person who remains hidden and communicates with the Shi'a community through deputies can be considered the rightful imam.

The Zaydi imam is also required to possess high moral character and religious learning. A person who does not possess all these requirements cannot be recognized as a full imam; there are thus lesser imams focused only on war or on learning. Leaders whose political and intellectual strength is only enough to keep the Zaydi religious claim alive are called *da'i*s, a term shared by the third Shi'a sect, the Isma'ilis. The high standards required of a Zaydi imam combined with the concept of the *da'i* allows for the possibility of an age to exist without an imam, when the community is lead by *da'i*s as representatives of the imam. Zaydi Shi'ism never gained a truly large following when compared with the other Shi'a sects; in modern times it is almost entirely limited to Yemen.

Twelvers

Those members of the Shi'a community who did not accept Zayd as the rightful imam remained in agreement for two more generations. The sixth imam of this group, the great scholar Ja'far as-Sādiq (c. 700–765 CE), is especially important because he has such a great reputation that the Sunnis also respect him. Al-Sādiq is believed to have written a great deal on theology and law, and the major Shi'a school of law is called Ja'fari because of him.

After the death of Ja'far as-Sādiq, this Shi'a group divided into two, the first recognizing Ja'far as-Sādiq's elder son Ismā'īl (c. 721–755 CE) as the rightful leader, leading to their being called Ismā'īlis. The second group followed Ja'far as-Sādiq's younger son, Musa (d. 799 CE). This latter sect continued following a chain of imams until the twelfth in succession from 'Alī, Muhammad al-Mahdī al-Hujjah, vanished around 874. His followers believed that he had gone into a form of supernatural concealment and would return as the Messiah at the end of the world. This meant that he was the final imam, and as a result his followers came to be known as "Twelver Shi'a" believers.

Twelver Shi'a believers have a complex theory concerning the nature of the imam, which derives from the writings of the sixth imam, Ja'far as-Sādiq. According to this belief, there is an imam in every age who represents God on Earth. This imam designates his successor by a system called *nass*. The system involves giving the imam-designate a body of knowledge that contains both the

Shi'a Practices

In addition to reciting the Qur'an, Shi'a Muslims often gather to recite long prayers from Muhammad and the imams. One famous prayer is called the Prayer of Kumayl (Du'a Kumayl). It was narrated by 'Alī ibn Abī Tālib, whom Shi'a Muslims recognize as the first imam, and they recite it on Thursday nights. Following is the beginning of the Prayer of Kumayl:

O Allah! Bless Muhammad and his progeny.

O Allah! I beseech Thee by Thy mercy which encompasses all things / And by Thy power by which Thou overcometh all things and submit to it all things and humble before it all things / And by Thy might by which Thou hast conquered all things / And by Thy majesty against which nothing can stand up

And by Thy grandeur which prevails upon all things / And by Thy authority which is exercised over all things / And by Thy own self that shall endure forever after all things have vanished / And by Thy Names which manifest Thy power over all things / And by Thy knowledge which pervades all things / And by the light of Thy countenance which illuminates everything O Thou who art the light!

O Thou who art the most holy! O Thou who existed before the foremost! O Thou who shall exist after the last!

O Allah! Forgive me my such sins as would affront my continency / O Allah! Forgive me my such sins as would bring down calamity

O Allah! Forgive me my such sins as would change divine favours (into disfavours) / O Allah! Forgive me my such sins as would hinder my supplication / O Allah! Forgive me such sins as bring down misfortunes (or afflictions) / O Allah! Forgive my such sins as would suppress hope

O Allah! Forgive every sin that I have committed and every error that I have erred / O Allah! I endeavour to draw myself nigh to Thee through Thy invocation / And I pray to Thee to intercede on my behalf / And I entreat Thee by Thy benevolence to draw me nearer to Thee / And grant me that I should be grateful to Thee and inspire me to remember and to invoke Thee . . .

Translated by William Chattick in The Supplication of Kumayl. 'Alī ibn Abī Tālib.

outer and the inner meaning of the Qur'an, which is not possessed by any other human being.

The institution of the imam is a covenant between God and human beings, and all Twelver Shi'a believers are required to acknowledge and follow the imam of their age. There is a hadith tradition popular in Shi'a circles that states: "Whoever dies without having known and recognized the imam of his time dies as a disbeliever." Imams are believed to be proofs of God on Earth, and their words are the words of God. The imam of the time is a witness for the people and a doorway through which they can reach God. According to most Shi'a sect members, the imam is believed to be immune from sin or error, and therefore serves as a perfect guide for a virtuous, religious life.

Following the disappearance of the twelfth imam, the Shi'a community was led by *wakil* (envoys) acting on behalf of the imam, who asserted that they were in direct contact with him and were simply communicating the orders of the imam to Shi'a society. When the fourth *wakil* died in 939 CE, the institution of having an envoy representing the imam in the community ended. The period from then on came to be known as the Greater Occultation (concealment), as distinct from the earlier Lesser Occultation. During the Greater Occultation, which continues into current time, Twelver Shi'a Islam developed an elaborate system of clerical education and a formal clergy that took care of the religious needs of the Shi'a community in the absence of the imam. The highest rank of this clergy is believed to be inspired by the imam and is given the right to engage in independent reasoning, or *ijtihad*. In actual fact, since the sixteenth century CE, when Twelver Shi'a Islam became the official religion of Iran and emerged as the most popular form of Shi'a Islam in the world, Shi'a clerics have been somewhat conservative in their exercise of *ijtihad*. For all practical purposes, they act similarly to the way Sunni scholars do in the study of law, except, of course, that a Shi'a scholar is bound by the Shi'a canon as opposed to Sunni belief.

Ismā'īlis

Some Shi'a believers maintained that Ismā'īl, not his younger brother Musa, was the rightful seventh imam. They believed this despite the fact that Ismā'īl died before his father, Ja'far as-Sādiq. According to Ismā'īli doctrine, before dying, Ismā'īl designated his son Muhammad ibn Ismā'īl as his successor, and the line of imams continued with him.

Very little is known about the doctrines of the early supporters of the leadership of Isma'il and his son Muhammad. Most knowledge concerning their beliefs is reconstructed on the basis of later Isma'ili works. A fundamental feature of their thought was the division of all knowledge into two levels: *zahir*, an outer, apparent, exoteric one; and *batin*, an inner, hidden, esoteric one. The outer, *zahir* level consists of the commonly accepted and understood divinely revealed scriptures and the religious laws as they are laid out in these scriptures. This level of knowledge changes with every prophet and every scripture. The inner, *batin* level is what is concealed under the words of the scriptures and their laws. This hidden truth is their deeper, real meaning and is unchanging. It can only be made apparent through a process of interpretation that can only be carried out by someone who already possesses this knowledge. This special person would be the imam or one of his deputies.

One of the most interesting aspects of Isma'ili thought is the concept of cyclical time. According to this belief, history goes through a cycle of seven eras, each inaugurated by a prophet who publicly announces his message using a scripture. The first six of these prophets are Adam, Noah, Abraham, Moses, Jesus, and Muhammad. These prophets are accompanied by a silent companion who is the guardian of the hidden dimension of the scripture. The silent companions corresponding to the six prophets listed above are Seth, Shem, Ishmael, Aaron, Peter, and 'Ali. Each prophetic pair is followed by a series of seven imams, and the seventh becomes the public or vocal prophet of the next cycle. Thus, in the prophetic cycle of Jesus, Muhammad was the seventh imam, who also functioned as the public prophet of the next cycle. In the cycle of Muhammad, Muhammad ibn Isma'il was the seventh imam, and he will return at some point in the future to serve as the public prophet of his own prophetic cycle (the seventh), and bring the entire cycle of seven to an end and our world with it. Until his return, Isma'ilis believe that the hidden *batin* knowledge should be kept secret and only be revealed to initiated believers on an oath that they will not reveal these secrets to outsiders.

The Isma'ilis became extremely powerful in North Africa in the tenth century CE and founded a dynasty known as the Fatimids. For a brief period, the Fatimids posed a threat to the absolute political authority of the Sunni caliphs of the Abbasid dynasty (750–1258), which was based in Baghdad and had succeeded the Umayyads in most Islamic lands of the time. The great city of Cairo was founded by these Isma'ilis in the tenth century, as

Topics for Further Study

Abraham

Empire

Moses

Time, Conceptions of

ƒātima (c. 616–633 CE)

ƒātima, the daughter of Muhammad and Khadijah, married 'Alī, Muhammad's close companion, and they had two sons and a daughter (Hasan, Husayn, and Zaynab). Fātima was extremely close to her father: she accompanied him on important occasions including the surrender of Mecca; she also took care of him after he was wounded at the Battle of Uhud that took place near Medina in 625 CE. She died only a few months after Muhammad, and many people believe she actually died of grief. Fātima is the most famous of Muhammad's daughters largely because she was the wife of 'Alī and the mother of Muhammad's grandchildren. There is a famous account in which Muhammad is said to have gathered Fātima and her family under his cloak and referred to them as his own family. This event is one of the major pieces of evidence that the Shi'a sect uses to justify its belief in the right of 'Alī and Fātima's descendants to lead the *ummah* (community). Fātima is so central to Shi'a Islam that a major Islamic dynasty, the Fatimids, claimed descent from her and took her name.

was Cairo's famous university, al-Azhar. This university later became one of the most important centers of Sunni learning, and it continues in that role today.

Over the centuries, Ismā'īlism has split into a number of different sects. The most important division occurred at the end of the eleventh century between those who believed that Nizar (d. 1095) was the rightful imam and those who felt he lacked the moral standing to be the leader and that the real imam was Nizar's brother al-Musta'li (d. 1101). The ruling powers of the Fatimid Empire supported the religious claims of al-Musta'li, and the followers of Nizar were forced to flee territories controlled by the Fatimids or else hide for fear of persecution.

The Fatimid Empire was destroyed by the rise to power of another Sunni dynasty, but not before Ismā'īli scholars patronized by the Fatimids had left a lasting impact on Islamic philosophy and mysticism. The followers of Nizar found refuge among the mountainous regions of Syria and Iran, where they began a campaign of intense missionary activity among the Sunni and Twelver Shi'a population of the region. They also conducted a kind of guerrilla war against the Sunni government and the Christian crusader states that existed in Lebanon and Palestine at that time.

The Nizari Ismā'īli community was governed from a fortress called Rock of Alamut, located in the mountains of northern Iran. Rock of Alamut fell to the Mongols when they invaded Iran in the middle of the thirteenth century, and after that the Nizari Ismā'īli community became widely dispersed and divided into several more subsects. One of these subsects, called the Qasimshahis, continued in Iran, where their imam became involved in regional politics in the eighteenth century. In recognition of his loyalty, the nineteenth-century Iranian monarch gave the then imam of the Qasimshahis the title of Agha Khan, which translates roughly as "Honorable Lord," a title that has been kept by his descendants.

Ismā'īlis remain an extremely fragmented and dispersed collection of Shi'a sects. The strongest concentration of Ismā'īlis belonging to the Nizari line is in Pakistan, particularly in the northern mountainous regions of Hunza and Gilgit, although smaller populations are found in India, Iran, and Afghanistan. The Ismā'īlis of the line of al-Musta'li are concentrated around the Arabian Sea, on the western coast of India, and in Pakistan and Yemen. Each Ismā'īli group continues to believe in its own imam, although these figures do not wield the kind of religious authority they did in the eleventh and twelfth centuries.

Mystical Islam—Sufism

Sufism is an umbrella term for a variety of philosophical, social, and literary phenomena occurring within Muslim society. In its narrowest sense, it refers to a number of schools of Islamic mystical philosophy and theology, to the phenomenon of religious orders and guilds that have exerted considerable influence over the development of Islamic politics and society, and to the varied expressions of popular piety and shrine cults found throughout the Islamic regions of the world. In a wider sense, Sufism is often seen as the spiritual muse behind much premodern verse in Muslim literature, the idiom of much popular Islamic piety, the primary social arena open to women's religious participation, and a major force in the conversion of people to Islam in Africa and Asia.

Sufi Orders

The Sufi orders served as educational institutions that fostered the religious sciences, music, and decorative arts. Their leaders sometimes functioned as theologians and judges, combining scholastic and charismatic forms of leadership. They also challenged the power of the legal and theological establishment. In

Quick Facts: Islamic Mystical Poetry

With the spread of Islam, the Islamic mystical tradition flourished and began to be expressed in a new form: mystical poetry. Unlike other spiritual poems, the mystical poems used a special metaphorical language describing divine intoxication with spiritual wine in the tavern of mystical love. One renowned poet is Jalāl ad-Din ar-Rūmī, who became the best-selling poet in North America in the twenty-first century, despite the fact that he lived in the thirteenth century and wrote in Persian. One of Rumi's poems follows:

I Am Wind, You Are Fire

O you who've gone on pilgrimage—
   where are you, where, oh where?
Here, here is the Beloved!
   Oh come now, come, oh come!
Your friend, he is your neighbor,
   he is next to your wall—
You, erring in the desert—
   what air of love is this?
If you'd see the Beloved's
   form without any form—
You are the house, the master,
   You are the Kaaba, you! . . .
Where is a bunch of roses,
   if you would be this garden?
Where, one soul's pearly essence
   when you're the Sea of God?
That's true— and yet your troubles
   may turn to treasures rich—
How sad that you yourself veil
   the treasure that is yours!

Translated by Annemarie Schimmel

---

modern times (as in earlier times), the Sufi orders have been praised for their capacity to serve as channels of religious reform while being criticized for a lack of respect for Islamic law and for fostering ignorance and superstition in order to maintain their control over the community.

Origins

The origins of Sufism lie in an informal movement of personal piety that emerged in the first century of Islam. This movement, which was too informal and unformed to be called a school, was characterized by an emphasis on prayer, asceticism, and withdrawal from society. The earliest Sufis lived in caves or simple huts on the edges of the cities, and they wore coarse woolen robes as a sign of their religious beliefs. The term Sufism derives from the practice of wearing wool.

(*Suf* is the Arabic word for "wool.") The earliest Sufis also spent almost all their waking hours in prayer, and they frequently engaged in acts of self-mortification, such as starving themselves or staying up the entire night, as a form of religious exercise. They also lived in complete poverty, having renounced their connections to the world and possessing little other than the clothes on their backs. A large percentage of these early Sufis were women; several are revered to this day, such as Rābi'ah al-'Adawīyah.

The early Sufi practices of asceticism and the wearing of wool are shared by Christian mystics and ascetics of the same period, and it is very likely that the Sufis adopted these practices after observing the Christian ascetics who lived with them in Syria and Palestine. Sufis, however, place the origins of their movement and its practices in the Qur'an and in the life of Muhammad. They

Rābi'ah al-'Adawīyah (c. 713–801 CE)

Rābi'ah al-'Adawīyah is the most famous woman Sufi mystic in Islamic history. She was the fourth daughter (*Rabi'ah* means "fourth") born to an extremely poor family in the city of Basra (in modern-day Iraq). She fell into slavery as a child and spent most of her youth as the property of a cruel master. But her deep piety and asceticism convinced him to free her, after which she moved to a cave in the hills outside Basra and spent the rest of her life in devotion.

Rābi'ah al-'Adawīyah's religious practice emphasized a love for and complete devotion to God. She is most famous for having prayed to God that if she worshipped him because she feared hell, he should throw her into hell; if she worshipped him out of a desire for paradise, he should banish her from paradise; but if she worshipped him for his own sake, then he should not withhold from her his eternal beauty. A similar sentiment is apparent in a famous poem ascribed to her: "I love you with two loves, the love of desire / And the love which is your due." Many miracles are ascribed to Rābi'ah al-'Adawīyah, and she remains a model of the Muslim who is completely devoted to God with absolutely no motivation other than a pure love for him.

are quick to observe that Muhammad lived an extremely simple, almost ascetic life, and that he often withdrew from Mecca to meditate in a cave. Indeed, it was while meditating in this way that he received his first revelation. Sufis therefore see their practices as an imitation of Muhammad, and their goal as similar to the one he achieved in his relationship with God.

The goal of Sufi practices is to have an intimate, personal experience of God in this world. According to Islamic belief, all Muslims will have a direct encounter with God after they die (opinions differ on what this means), but Sufis do not wish to wait and instead want to have the encounter with God before they die. This desire is expressed in a saying attributed to the Prophet and very popular in Sufi circles that encourages Muslims to "Die before you die."

This direct experience with God is considered so overwhelming that it is indescribable and can only be spoken about in metaphors. The most commonly used metaphors are those of falling in love and of being intoxicated with wine. These images are frequently encountered in Sufi literature, particularly in the vast amount of Sufi poetry that has been written in all Islamic languages to try to express the indescribable joy that Sufis experience through their relationship with God.

Union with God

The concept of union with God is expressed in many different ways, and the problems involved in understanding how a mortal human being could unite with the omnipotent, omniscient deity who is unlike us in every way has been the basis of much debate in Sufi philosophical circles. The union with God is normally called *fana*, which literally means "destruction" or "annihilation." This relates to the Sufi belief that the final stage in an individual's spiritual development is losing any consciousness of individual identity and only being aware of the identity of God. In effect, God's identity replaces the identity of the Sufi.

A famous Sufi named Mansūr al-Hallāj (c. 858–922) expressed this feeling of loss of self when he cried out, "I am Divine Truth!" He was killed for making such seemingly blasphemous utterances in public, although what he was trying to communicate was the message that he, Mansūr al-Hallāj, no longer existed as an individual, because his consciousness had been replaced by the consciousness of God. Similar controversial statements have been made by many Sufis who were attempting to use shocking or paradoxical speech to get their message across to the rest of their society.

Quick Facts: Asceticism

Asceticism, or the sacrificing of worldly pleasures in favor of spiritual enlightenment, is common to many major world religions. For instance, in Hindu history, a group of ascetics reacted against the Brahmins, or priests, who controlled the common people's access of religious texts and knowledge. Thus, these ascetics retreated to the woods to seek spiritual knowledge, and their efforts resulted in the Hindu holy texts, the Upanishads. Prince Siddhārtha Gautama, who later founded Buddhism, was inspired by an ascetic to leave his royal family and wealth to seek the truth. Christianity's Jesus of Nazareth was often known to challenge his mind and body by subjecting himself to the extreme conditions of the desert of Judaea for prolonged periods.

Sufis disagree over whether the final spiritual goal of Sufism is to lose personal identity completely in the identity of God, or to reach a stage where petty human concerns no longer prevent the believer from seeing the world in its true nature; in other words, to see things the way God sees them. A common metaphor for the first approach is to describe the Sufi's individuality as a drop that vanishes into the ocean; it does not cease to exist entirely, for it is now part of the vastness of the sea; it only ceases to exist insofar as it is an individual drop. The view that the individual sees things more clearly depicts the human heart (the seat of the intellect in medieval Islamic thought just as it was in medieval Christian thought) as a mirror that is normally dirty. The dirt or tarnish on the mirror is humans' everyday concerns and petty desires. Through engaging in mystical exercises, believers effectively polish the mirrors of their hearts and cleanse them to the point where they can accurately reflect the light of God.

The Sufi Path

Sufis believe that the average human being is unable to understand the true nature of the world and of spirituality because most people are too involved in the petty concerns of everyday life to see things as they really are. The quest for

Can people gain religious enlightenment without removing themselves from the constraints of their daily lives? How does the starkness of asceticism enable spiritual growth? Can you think of any modern-day ascetics?

spiritual understanding in Sufism is seen as a path each Sufi must travel under the guidance of a teacher or master. This path has many stations, and their numbers and names vary depending on the school of Sufi thought. Usually the first stage on the Sufi path is repentance. The Sufi is expected to repent all bad deeds and take a vow to avoid all earthly pleasures; this includes activities that are both permissible and forbidden according to Islamic law.

After repenting, the Sufi abandons the things of this world, divesting him- or herself of earthly belongings. This means giving up property and detaching the self from friends and family. After doing so, the Sufi enters a monastery or convent and becomes fully devoted to the difficult task of getting rid of earthly concerns. In actual fact, it is extremely difficult, however, to truly abandon past habits and eradicate all family attachments, so the process of divestment often takes a long time and requires strict, meditational exercises under the master's direction. A Sufi often thus begins the exercises associated with the next stage before completely transcending the previous stage. For example, the individual might perform the exercises associated with divestment while still trying to truly repent previous habits.

Meditation (*Zikr*)

The Sufi path, which consists of slowly ridding the self of worldly concerns, relies on meditation to accomplish its goals. The various Sufi forms of mediation are called *zikr* (or *dhikr*), literally meaning "repetition," "remembrance," "utterance," or "mentioning." The term appears several times in the Qur'an and urges Muslims to frequently remember their Lord ("do *zikr* of him"). The most basic level of *zikr* consists of repeating one of God's names. In Islam, God is believed to have many names that describe some aspect of his nature. Ninety-nine names are considered special and are called the "Most Beautiful Names."

Sufis recite one or another of these names (e.g., Qa'im, meaning "eternal," Khaliq, meaning "creator," or Rahim, meaning "merciful") as many times as their master orders.

The most frequently used name of God is Allah, which Sufis believe to be the best name. The purpose of reciting these names is to fulfill the master's command and to concentrate fully on what the Sufi is doing so that the individual loses all self-awareness. The Sufi repeats the *zikr* formula (in this case, a name of God) enough times so that it permeates the individual's entire being and continues to be repeated in the individual's heart even if the person ceases to actively engage in *zikr*. This is a way of eradicating worldly concerns and self-absorption and of focusing on God.

Some *zikr* exercises involve repeating other, longer formulas, while some involve complicated methods of breath control. A relatively simple *zikr* exercise involving breath control requires the Sufi to say a bisyllabic name of God out loud, inhaling on the first syllable (while saying it aloud) and exhaling on the second syllable. This is called the "sawing *zikr*," because the distinctive sound made by speaking while inhaling and exhaling resembles the noise made by a saw as it cuts through wood. Other forms are more complicated, such as reciting the formula, "There is no god but God" in a long breath broken up into five beats. Such complex meditational exercises are difficult to learn without a master, and they only became popular after the master-disciple relationship had evolved into hierarchical Sufi orders, called *tariqa*s ("paths").

Organized Sufism

By the thirteenth century, Sufism had become organized into orders. Their origins stem from the social environment of the medieval Islamic world, where trade guilds evolved into important organizations that provided working-class people with security and a sense of belonging. Educational and legal institutions were also formalized by this time, as was the relationship between the government and the theological and legal scholars. It is therefore not surprising that Sufism would also take an organized form and compete for social legitimacy and authority with other religious movements and institutions.

The earliest Sufi orders were simple organizations made up of the disciples of a particular master; after these disciples became accomplished Sufis, they felt that they owed their spiritual standing to their teachers and so imparted his teachings to their own students. This second generation of students felt that they belonged to the spiritual lineage of that first master and his *tariqa*.

By the fourteenth century, Sufi orders had become formally organized. Someone who wanted to become a Sufi would visit a master from the desired order and request to be accepted as a student. The master would often turn the applicant away many times before finally accepting the person. The aspiring Sufi would then be put through an initiation process that included performing menial

Jalāl ad-Din ar-Rūmī (Rumi; c. 1207–1273 CE)

Rumi is one of the greatest mystical poets of the Persian language. He is often referred to by his full name, Jalāl ad-Din ar-Rūmī, or simply as Mawlānā, Mevlana, or Mawlavi, all titles of respect.

Rumi was born in the Central Asian city of Balkh (now in northern Afghanistan), but moved as a young man to the city of Konya in Turkey, where his father was a professor. After his father's death, Rumi took over his father's teaching position. His life was utterly transformed with the arrival in Konya of a wandering Sufi mystic named Shams al-Din of Tabriz (d. 1247). Rumi saw Shams as a source of great mystical knowledge and a window through which he could contemplate God. He became so obsessed with Shams that he began to neglect his students, who conspired to get rid of Shams, possibly by killing him. Instead of making him return to his teaching duties, the disappearance of Shams caused Rumi to devote himself even more fully to the world of Sufi mysticism. He began to write mystical poetry, most of it in a collection dedicated to Shams. He is equally famous for his book-length poem, the *Masnavi-ye Ma'navi*, which is full of advice and allegorical and moralistic tales.

Rumi was an ecstatic Sufi whose mystical feelings of joy caused him to whirl around in dance. His followers, known as the Mevlevis, adopted his dancing as a form of meditation. This ritual is so distinctive in European societies that the Mevlevis came to be known as the Whirling Dervishes. The Mevlevis were very influential in the Ottoman Empire (c. 1300–1922), where many classical musicians and poets belonged to this Sufi order.

tasks before being formally recognized as a full member of the order. Admission was normally a ceremonial occasion when new members would be given robes or hats signifying their new status.

Many Sufi orders have been extremely important in the development of Islamic Muslim society: they had major scholars and philosophers developing their ideas, and major government figures often belonged to them, which meant that the Sufi orders had influence over the official policies of the kingdom. Three such orders that deserve special attention are the Chishti, Naqshbandi, and Mevlevi.

Chishti Order

The Chisthi order is named after Khaja Mu'in al-Din Chishti (d. 1235) who was from a town in Afghanistan called Chisht. After finishing his education in Afghanistan and Central Asia, he settled in the town of Ajmer in India, where he taught a large number of disciples, many of whom were extremely influential and had disciples of their own. These disciples of Khaja Chishti opened Chishti centers in provincial towns all over India; they also had many rulers, princes, and princesses as their disciples, and the order rapidly became the most influential in India.

The Chishti order has as its *zikr* a particular kind of musical performance called *qavvali* in which a group of musicians sing religious songs set to a rhythmic beat. It is worth noting that it is not the musicians who are engaging in *zikr* but their audience, who use the music as a meditational device. In the twentieth century, *qavvali* became a popular musical form and has been spread in the West by such artists as the Pakistani singer Nusrat Fateh Ali Khan (1948–1997).

Naqshbandi Order

The Naqshbandi order is named after a Central Asian Sufi scholar from the city of Bukhara in Uzbekistan, Baha al-Din Naqshband (1318–1389). He actually belonged to an important Sufi organization called, in Persian, Silsila-yi Khajagan ("Chain of Masters"), which is so similar to the Naqshbandi order that it is questionable why later generations saw him as the founder of a new order.

The Naqshandi order is famous for its involvement in society. Unlike many other

Topics for Further Study

Dance and Military Drill

Music—Overview

Mysticism

Rumi

Sufis, Naqshbandis believe that a Sufi should not withdraw from society but should pursue his spiritual goals while fulfilling all his social responsibilities. The Naqshbandis hold eight principles to be central to their order and trace them back to the most famous in the Chain of Masters, Ghijduvani (d. 1220). These are awareness while breathing, watching one's steps, journeying within, solitude within human society, recollection, restraining one's thoughts, watching one's thoughts, and concentration on the divine.

The order enjoyed considerable influence in India, where it was introduced from Central Asia in the middle of the sixteenth century. A generation later, a scholar named Ahmad Sirhindī (1593–1624) had a tremendous impact on the development of the Naqshbandi order, not just in India but on its international spread from that time forward. Sirhindī held the view that a period of moral and social decay had plagued Islamic society since the death of Muhammad, and said that it could only be reversed by the arrival of a religious renewer. Although he never made the explicit claim that he was this awaited renewer, his teachings give an undeniable impression that he saw himself as pivotal in the course of human religious history. His followers named him the "Renewer (Mujaddid) of the Second Millennium," and the branch of the Naqshbandi order deriving from him became known as the Mujaddidi school and has come to dominate the Naqshbandi order.

Naqshbandi figures were very important in religious reform movements in the eighteenth and nineteenth centuries, particularly in India and Central Asia where Muslims were fighting British and Russian colonialism, respectively. Toward the end of the eighteenth century in India, two members of the Naqshbandi order started a new, modern Sufi movement called the Tariqa-yi Muhammadiya ("Path of Muhammad"). It essentially was a mystical interpretation of a legally conformist form of Sunni Islam that derived a great deal from Naqshbandi attitudes toward the law and the individual's place in society.

The Naqshbandi order continues to be extremely important as a force of reform in some Muslim regions, particularly among Turkish-speaking people. Naqshbandis were at the forefront of religious resistance to the Soviet Union and now provide education and social services in many of the Central Asian and Caucasian countries that emerged after the Soviet Union's collapse.

Mevlevi Order

The primarily Turkish Mevlevi order was well known in Europe because of its distinctive *zikr* ritual in which dancers called Whirling Dervishes rotate in precise rhythms. The order derives its name from Jalāl ad-Din ar-Rūmī (c. 1207–1273), who is called Mevlana in Turkish. Rumi was born in the Central Asian city of Balkh, where his father was an important religious scholar and Sufi master. Rumi moved to Turkey in 1219, when his father was appointed professor of legal thought at a university in Konya, the seat of the Seljuk dynasty (1038–1157). Rumi inherited this post after his father's death.

The defining moment in Rumi's life occurred in 1244 with the arrival of a wandering mystic named Shams ad-Din of Tabriz. Rumi began to spend all his time with Shams, whom he saw as a means of gaining access to the mystical knowledge of God. Shams was sent away (and probably killed) by Rumi's students, at which point Rumi withdrew from public life and devoted himself entirely to the guidance of Sufi disciples. It is likely that a Sufi order gathered around Rumi while he was still alive and at some later point came to be known as the Mevlevi order.

Whirling dervishes dance to the music of flutes, tambourines, and violins, in Turkey, August 1920. Library of Congress, American National Red Cross Collection.

Mevlevi Meditation

The two most distinctive features of the Mevlevi order are its lengthy process of initiation and the importance its members give to music and dance in their *zikr* practices. The Mevlevi meditational exercise, called *sama*, involves reciting a number of prayers and hymns. After that, the participants make several rounds of the hall, in a dance with their arms extended sideways, the right palm facing up and the left down. They whirl counterclockwise, using their left feet as pivots. According to Mevlevi teachings, the upturned right hand symbolizes the mystic's receipt of divine grace, while the downturned left hand implies that what is received from God is passed on to humanity.

The Mevlevi order has emphasized art and culture since Rumi's day and has always encouraged court poets and musicians. Its importance to the development of the culture of the Ottoman Empire (c. 1300–1922) cannot be overemphasized. Many important Ottoman poets and composers were Mevlevis. This connection with the arts is still important, and the Mevlevi order is popular with young musicians and poets in modern Turkey.

Philosophy and Theology

As a prophet, Muhammad's role was more that of a preacher than a theologian. The Qur'an, however, brings up many philosophical and theological questions regarding the nature of God, God's relationship to the world, the problem of evil, and the place occupied by human beings in the divine plan for the universe. As the Muslim-ruled territory expanded to absorb new cultures, many new philosophical questions emerged. Some of these issues were already being discussed in the newly converted territories; others were brought up by the theological debates that occurred as Islam came into competition with Christianity and Zoroastrianism, which were the major religions of that region. Still others emerged as a result of political and social crises that plagued the early Muslim community.

Kalam (Theology)

The term most commonly used for theology in the Islamic community is *kalam*, which literally means "speech" or "dialectic." This gives a clear sense of the fact that Islamic theology emerged in an environment where theological issues were being publicly debated. *Kalam* is distinct from Islamic philosophy in that the philosophical tradition derived consciously and directly from Greek (and to a lesser extent, Persian) thought. This is clear even from the word used for philosophy, which is *falsafa*.

Many of the major questions that were discussed in the earliest Islamic theological circles arose out of the political crises that followed the assassinations of the caliphs Umar, 'Uthmān ibn 'Affān, and 'Alī, and from the civil wars that resulted in the division between the Sunni and Shi'a sects. The main questions dealt with who the rightful leader was of the community and what the status was of a believer who committed a grave sin (since the killers of the early caliphs were all Muslims). As theological schools grew within Muslim society, the questions being debated became more theoretical and abstract. The main issues concerned the relationship between God's omnipotence and human responsibility. This led to more-abstract discussions of the nature of God and of how human beings gained the ability to differentiate between right and wrong and commit good and bad actions.

Schools of Thought

Following the murder of 'Uthmān ibn 'Affān and the emergence of sectarian divisions, four major schools of thought emerged, representing the spectrum of Islamic theological opinions. The first, the Qadariyya, was the most actively opposed to the Umayyad dynasty. The Qadariyya believed that human beings have such extensive power over their actions that they can determine the commission and outcome of their acts. It is from this belief in human ability or determination (*qudra*) that the Qadariyya gets its name. Since human beings had complete freedom of action, works were considered to be a perfect mirror of a person's belief and an integral path of faith. Thus, in the understanding of the Qadariyya, someone who committed a grave sin must be a disbeliever.

The second group is called the Jabriyya and is the direct opposite of the original Qadariyya. The Jabriyya believed that divine compulsion (*jabr*) created human actions and that human beings had absolutely no freedom in committing good or bad actions. Since God was the direct source of all acts, a human being could not be held responsible for committing a grave sin and therefore would still be considered a Muslim.

The Murji'a occupied a position in between the Qadariyya and the Jabriyya. They believed that it was not possible for human beings to pass judgment over the status of another human being's faith. Instead, they believed that a grave sinner's future was held in suspense awaiting God's decision. This concept of suspense, from which the Arabic word *murji'a* is derived, is based on a verse from the Qur'an (9:106): "There are others, held in suspense for the command of Allah, whether He will punish them, or turn in mercy to them."

The last major group is called the Khawarij. This group held a strict belief that actions were the perfect mirror of an individual's faith. This idea was shared with the Qadariyya, the major difference being that the Khawarij were extremely active politically and constituted the first

Topics for Further Study

Religion and War

War and Peace—Overview

Islamic religious sect. They felt it was the duty of every true Muslim to depose, by force if necessary, any leader who had strayed from the correct path. They also believed that any Muslim male, regardless of whether he belonged to Muhammad's tribe of Quraysh or not, could be declared caliph as long as that person was of irreproachable moral character. The Khawarij had originally supported 'Alī in his competition with Mu'āwiyah, but when 'Alī agreed to human arbitration (as opposed to letting God make the decision on the battlefield), they deserted him and came to be distinct from his supporters, who became the Shi'a believers.

Mu'tazila and the Ash'ariyya Theological Schools

By the end of the eighth century CE, these early theological trends had developed to the point that full-fledged theological schools had emerged. The most famous is called the Mu'tazila, which rose for a brief period to be the official theological school of the Sunni world. This forty-year period in the middle of the ninth century CE is particularly important because, under the influence of the Mu'tazila, the Sunni world went through a period of crisis when many religious scholars and theologians were put on trial to see whether their beliefs agreed with those of the Mu'tazila. Being found guilty could have serious consequences, ranging from losing a job to imprisonment and, or rare occasions, death.

The major results of this "inquisition" were that the various theological positions among Muslims became much more defined and formal schools of thought formed. It also meant that when the official power of the Mu'tazila ended, they came to be seen as heretical and were themselves victims of discrimination and persecution. The school of theology that replaced the Mu'tazila is called the Ash'ariyya, named after a theologian named Abū al-Hasan al-Ash'ari (c. 873–c. 935 CE), who had originally belonged to the Mu'tazila but later abandoned it and became one of its greatest critics.

A good way of understanding the basic tenets of Islamic theology is to see how the Mu'tazila and Ash'ariyya disagreed on specific questions:

1. The Qur'an mentions many attributes describing God, such as "all-seeing," "merciful," "compassionate," and "just." God is also believed to be completely unlike human beings. Taken together, many people find it difficult to reconcile the concept of God being absolutely unlike human beings with the fact that we refer to God using adjectives (such as "com-

passionate" or "merciful") that are the same as those we use to describe a human being. This problem is even greater when the Qur'an speaks of things such as the "hand" of God or talks about his "throne," which implies that God sits, and in turn has a body. The Mu'tazila declared that all the attributes used to describe God are distinct from his essence. Since his essence is the only thing that exists eternally, his attributes are noneternal. The Ash'ariyya, in contrast, said that God does indeed have eternal attributes, such as knowledge, sight, and speech, by which he knows, sees, and speaks, but that these attributes are different from the ones human beings have.

2. Regarding the anthropomorphic attributes of God (such as his hands or face), the Mu'tazila declared that the attributes are completely symbolic and had to be interpreted metaphorically. The Ash'ariyya stated that the anthropomorphic attributes mentioned in the Qur'an are real, but we human beings are incapable of understanding their true meaning.

3. The Ash'ariyya stated that the Qur'an is God's speech. Since speech is an attribute of God, the Ash'ariyya view the Qur'an as being part of him and therefore eternal. As a result, according to their belief and that of the overwhelming majority of Muslims, the Qur'an is the eternal speech of God. In contrast, the Mu'tazila, on the basis of their belief that God's attributes are not part of him and therefore are not eternal, maintained that the Qur'an was not eternal.

4. The Qur'an promises human beings a vision of God in the afterlife. This is theologically problematic because Muslims generally believe that God has no body and cannot be seen. The Mu'tazila followed this logic very strictly, saying that since God cannot be seen physically, he cannot be seen in the afterlife either; therefore, this promise of the vision of God cannot be accurate. The Ash'ariyya stated that the vision of God in the world to come is real, but we do not understand what the nature of it will be.

5. The Ash'ariyya stressed God's omnipotence, declaring that both good and evil are willed by God. God created human actions as well as the ability to choose between right and wrong. Using this theory, which in Islamic philosophy is called the Doctrine of Acquisition, the Ash'ariyya successfully reconciled a belief in God's omnipotence with the desire to hold human beings accountable for their actions. The Mu'tazila, on the

other hand, insisted on complete human freedom and responsibility. They declared that God only wills good and neither wills nor creates evil. Human beings create their own acts and are completely responsible for all the evil things they do.

6. Based on their complex understanding of the relationship between human actions and the will of an omnipotent God, the Ash'ariyya maintained that any Muslim who commits a grave sin would still be considered a Muslim but would, nevertheless, be punished in hell. In contrast, the Mu'tazila argued that such persons would occupy a position somewhere between that of belief and disbelief, since they had freely declared themselves to be Muslims, but had freely committed an evil act that showed that their faith could not be perfect.

Human Reason

The differences between the Mu'tazila and the Ash'ariyya, which became the dominant school of theology among Sunni Muslims, can be seen as pertaining to different understandings of the power of human reason. The Ash'ariyya acknowledged that human beings have some degree of free will and power of reasoning, but they felt that these human abilities were extremely limited when compared with the omniscience and omnipotence of God. The Mu'tazila, however, held the (some say arrogant) belief in the powers of the human intellect and refused to accept that certain things lay beyond human understanding. Both positions have bases in the Islamic philosophical tradition from which Islamic theology derived many of its ideas.

Development of Islamic Philosophy

The Islamic philosophers emerged in an environment where they were heirs to the rich, philosophical tradition of the Greeks and Persians. As a result, they adopted the systems of thought developed by Aristotle, Plato, and the Neoplatonists. The big difference between the early Islamic philosophers and the theologians is that the theologians, though clearly influenced by earlier philosophers, did not consciously adopt pre-Islamic systems of thought, whereas Islamic philosophers did so wholeheartedly. This is readily apparent from their use of the term *falsafa* for philosophy.

Islamic Philosophers

Many thinkers were critically important to the development of Islamic philosophy. Four deserve special attention for the great impact they had on the development of thought in both the Islamic and medieval worlds: Al-Kindī, Al-Fārābī, Ibn Sīnā, and Al-Ghazālī.

Al-Kindī (d. c. 873 CE)

Yaqūb ibn Ishāq as-Sabah al-Kindī was of Arab origin, born in the city of Kufa, Iraq, where his father was the governor. He was extremely well educated and tried to absorb all the learning and culture of the time, becoming well versed in philosophy, medicine, geography, theology, and history. Al-Kindī was directly influenced by the major Greek philosophers and is responsible for importing many of their terms into Arabic, leading to their common use among Islamic philosophers. He believed in the essential compatibility of philosophy and theology and was closely associated with the Mu'tazila theological school; consequently he was persecuted and his library was temporarily confiscated.

Al-Fārābī (d. c. 950 CE)

Abū Nasr al-Fārābī is widely considered an outstanding Islamic philosopher and is often referred to as the "Second Teacher," the "First Teacher" being Aristotle. He was born in Central Asia but came to Baghdad (in modern-day Iraq) early in life because his father was an officer in the Turkish palace guard of the caliph. He was educated in Baghdad and later moved to Aleppo (now part of Syria), where he joined the group of scholars who were part of the court of the local ruler. Al-Fārābī's basic conviction was that philosophy had ended everywhere in the world except in the Islamic lands, where it had found a new home. He believed that human reason was superior to religious faith because philosophical truths, which are derived through reason, are universally valid, whereas religious truths rely on symbols that vary from society to society.

Ibn Sīnā (980–1037)

Abū 'Alī al-Husayn ibn 'Abd Allāh ibn Sīnā was a respected Islamic philosopher and physician. He was an extremely talented and precocious student who had outlearned his teachers by the time he was fourteen. From then on, he taught himself and actually learned certain sciences, in particular medicine and the natural sciences, without any teachers. His *Canon of Medicine* served as the basis of medical teaching and practice for seven centuries, not just in the Muslim world but also in Europe, where he was widely known by his Latin name, Avicenna.

Perhaps Ibn Sīnā's biggest philosophical contribution was an elaborate theory that demonstrated the philosophical necessity for the existence of God and how the physical world came into being through a process known as "emanation." (Emanation is distinct from the process of creation, which is the common religious understanding in Islam.) He explained many of these ideas in a famous allegorical work about a man who grows up alone on a desert island and, using only the power of his intellect and the evidence of the things he finds around him, rationally comes to understand the nature of the universe and the necessity of a supreme being. Ibn Sīnā's philosophical works also show a tendency toward mysticism, a trend that was becoming extremely popular in the Muslim world at this time. It was in the realm of Islamic mysticism that much of the later Islamic philosophical inquiry continued, making Ibn Sīnā the most revered of the classical Islamic philosophers.

Al-Ghazālī (d. 1111 CE)

Abu Hāmid Muhammad ibn Muhammad at-Tūsī al-Ghazālī is one of the most influential Islamic scholars. He spent the majority of his adult life as a professor of theology. At the height of his professorial career, in 1095, he suffered a severe emotional crisis that caused him to leave his job in Baghdad, return to his hometown, and devote himself to a life of contemplation. He eventually concluded that rational and philosophical inquiry can carry a person only so far, and that achieving complete understanding requires a leap of faith. This leap of faith was best achieved through mystical education, something commonly referred to as Sufism. Thus, Al-Ghazālī represents a turning point in Islamic thought as a rational scholar who sees the perfection of his education not in philosophy but in Sufism.

The Alexandrian School

As early as the eighth century CE, the Islamic Empire included cities such as Alexandria and Antioch, which had been important centers of Hellenistic learning from 332 to 30 BCE. Alexandria, in particular, is famous for being the home of an academy of learning. The academy's size had dwindled by Islamic times, but members of this school were later found in important Islamic cities such as Baghdad, where they had a great deal of influence on Islamic philosophers. The Persian Sasanid dynasty had its own philosophical academy in Gondeshapur that may have served as a model for institutes of learning in the eighth- and ninth-century Islamic societies.

Hellenistic philosophy and scientific literature were so highly regarded by the Muslims that, for a two-hundred-year period, Greek works were feverishly

Kitab ʃuwar al-kawakib (Book of the Constellations of the Fixed Stars, 964 CE) by astronomer ʿAbd al-Rahman ibn ʿUmar al-Sufi spurred research in astronomy and other scientific fields throughout Muslim and European societies.
Library of Congress.

translated into Arabic and provided the impetus for developments in many fields of learning in Muslim regions, particularly medicine and philosophy. These works were later translated from Arabic into Latin and became part of the learning of Christian Europe.

Quick Facts: Classical Islamic Science

Scientific discoveries flourished in the medieval Muslim world, perhaps due to the Qur'an's encouragement to ponder the natural world. Many of these advances soon found their way to Europe, where they left a lasting impact on the development of modern science. The medieval Muslim world featured advanced hospitals, universities, astronomical observatories, and public services. Muslim scientists made notable advances in navigation and cartography, while astronomers such as Abū 'Alī al-Hasan ibn al-Haytham (whose Latinized name is Alhazen) proposed that the Earth rotates on its axis. While several medieval Muslim astronomers also theorized that the Earth might actually orbit around the sun, the idea failed to catch on until Copernican times (fifteenth and sixteenth centuries). The many Islamic contributions to astronomy can be seen by the numerous Arabic names on any star map, such as Deneb ("the Tail") and "Rigel" ("the Foot").

As in Europe, many medieval Muslim thinkers were polymaths, specializing in several fields of science as well as philosophy and theology. Some of the best known are Ibn Sīnā (Latinized to Avicenna; 980–1037), who wrote a foundational work on medicine, and Muhammad ibn Mūsā al-Khwārizmī (c. 780–c. 850 CE), from whose name the English words "algebra" and "algorithm" derive.

Muslims also played a pivotal role in transmitting knowledge from other civilizations, such as the art of Chinese papermaking and the translation of Greco-Roman texts. Not only did medieval Muslims preserve these ancient texts, but they also engaged the ideas found in them—accepting some, rejecting others, and developing an elaborate system of comparative philosophy. To participate in this intellectual renaissance, European scholars translated numerous texts from the Muslim world from Arabic into Latin.

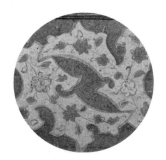

Teachings

Islam has a highly developed set of beliefs and rituals that are required of all pious Muslims. All of these have a basis in the Qur'an and the life of Muhammad and have been further developed by later theologians and legal scholars. This is why there is much variation in the way Muslims understand the cardinal points of their faith and how they observe its ritual requirements. Furthermore, like members of other religious communities, Muslims do not always observe every ritual, nor do they believe in particular dogmas of their religion in the same way.

The doctrines and rituals outlined here are from the Sunni sect, to which the overwhelming majority of Muslims belong. Other sects, particularly the Twelver Shi'a sect, believe in much the same things as the Sunnis do and practice their rituals in similar ways; nevertheless, there are differences.

Pillars of Faith

In the early development of Islamic doctrine during the eighth and ninth centuries CE, several scholars wrote creedal documents outlining what an individual is required to believe in order to be considered a Muslim. Such creedal documents varied considerably in their details, although they retained a central focus on the unity of God, revelation, and prophecy. Over time, these doctrines became formalized into lists, sometimes referred to as "Pillars of Faith" to parallel the "Pillars of Practice" (described later). Many Muslims hold that a person is required to believe in five cardinal points: divine unity, prophecy, revelation, angelic agency, and the existence of an afterlife.

Divine Unity

All Muslims are required to believe in the oneness of God. This God, normally known by the Arabic name Allah, is unique and eternal. He exists in and of himself and has no needs. Allah, by his own choosing, created the universe and all

63

Iznik, Turkey, is well known for the ceramics made there during the sixteenth century CE, such as this tile panel with flowers. Louvre Museum, Collection of Albert Sorlin-Dorigny; purchase, 1895.

that exists within it. He created human beings and gave them the capacity to do good as well as evil and the ability to choose between the two. Human beings can choose to know God through his attributes (such as mercy, justice, compassion, and wrath), but the ultimate essence of God remains unknowable. According to Islamic understanding, God has no body and is unlike anything in the created world. Furthermore, it is a very grave sin to consider anything as an equal or companion of God.

Prophecy

The majority of Muslims believe that God has the wish to communicate with human beings, and that he uses prophets for this purpose. Prophets are of two types, the first being those who have a mission from God to warn their communities and acquaint them with God's will. Those in the second category, in addition to fulfilling all the functions of the first category, are also given a revealed scripture to convey to their communities. Muslims believe in a series of prophets that includes all the prophets mentioned in the Hebrew Bible as well as Jesus and Muhammad. Muhammad is considered the final prophet, and Muslims are not permitted to call anyone after him a prophet. Muslims consider Jesus to be the second-to-last prophet, who foretold the coming of Muhammad. The majority of Muslims also consider Jesus to be the Messiah, and they believe in the virgin birth. They do not, however, take this to mean that God was the father of Jesus, but rather that God performed a miracle by causing Mary to conceive without a biological father.

Revelation

Muslims believe that God uses his prophets to reveal scriptures to humanity. Four scriptures are recognized by Muslims: the Torah as revealed to Moses, the Psalms of David, the New Testament of Jesus, and the Qur'an of Muhammad. According to Muslim belief, God's message is eternal, and thus the substance of all these books is the same. Differences between them are explained using two theories. The first is that, after their revelation, earlier scriptures were tampered with by people who claimed to believe in them. The second explanation relies on a theory of human evolution, according to which God knew what he wished to teach humanity. Humanity, however, was not always ready for the full message. For this reason, God revealed his message in progressively more comprehensive versions, culminating in the Qur'an, which is the definitive version of God's message, valid until the end of civilization.

Muslims consider the possession of a scripture as central to their understanding of what constitutes a real religion. For this reason, whenever they encountered new religions (such as Hinduism or Buddhism) and wished to appreciate them as valid, in the same way that they consider Judaism and Christianity to be valid religions, they have tried to identify a scripture within

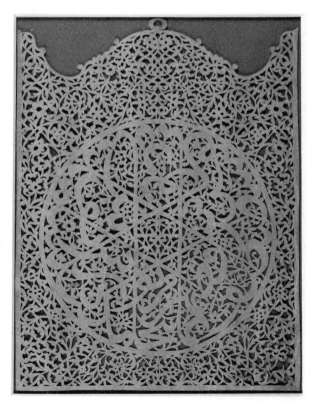

Découpage, or cut paper, became a popular method for making Ottoman *kalips* (calligraphic perforated sheets) during the sixteenth to nineteenth centuries CE; this panel was made in Ottoman Turkey in the eighteenth or nineteenth century.
Library of Congress.

those traditions. They do this even when the believers of these religions (such as Hinduism) do not believe their religion possesses a scripture on the Islamic, Jewish, or Christian model.

Angelic Agency

Muslims are supposed to believe that angels exist and that God uses them to perform his will. One of their duties is to watch over individual human beings and keep a record of all their actions. The most famous angel is Gabriel, who served as an intermediary between God and Muhammad in the revelation of the Qur'an. Another important figure is Iblis, who was the chief of angels but was punished for disobeying God. After being cast out of heaven, Iblis was turned into Satan and now rules hell, trying to tempt human beings away from the path of goodness. Many Muslims consider belief in angels to be the most difficult Pillar of Faith, and they explain them away as natural forces or different aspects of God's power.

Afterlife

Muslims are required to believe that our world will eventually end and that we will be judged and rewarded or punished in the afterlife according to our actions in this world. Judgment, reward, and punishment are central points in Islam, and its entire system of ethics is based on them. It is therefore no surprise that Islam has a highly developed system of eschatology (theory of the end of the world).

The central events of Islamic theology as believed by most Sunni and Shi'a followers involve a conflict between good and evil. Evil appears to be winning until the Mahdi ("Guide") comes and leads good people in a triumph against evil and brings about a time of peace and justice. According to Sunni belief, the Mahdi is an individual who either has not yet come to Earth or is the same person as the Messiah, whom the majority of Sunnis hold to be Jesus. In Twelver Shi'a belief, the twelfth imam will return as the Guide in the end-times.

A great deal of variation exists in popular beliefs concerning the end of the world. According to one version, the coming of doomsday is foretold by a number of signs, such as a growing struggle between good and evil, in which evil appears to be taking the upper hand. As the time approaches, the natural order of things is overturned so that the sun rises in the west rather than the east and

This image of a Muslim saint ascending is from
M. J. B. Silvestre's *Universal Palaeography: or,
Fac-Similes of Writings of All Nations and Periods*
(Frederic Madden, Trans.). (1850). London: Henry
Bohn.

the seas start to boil. Finally, a trumpet sounds, causing people to scatter in all directions. About this time, a monstrous beast rises and starts striking people with its mark. When things reach their darkest point, the Messiah (very commonly believed to be Jesus) returns and gathers up all virtuous people to await doomsday and resurrection. It is important to note that, according to the Qur'an, the world does not so much come to a complete end as it is utterly transformed. It is therefore possible for some Muslims to argue that the afterlife occurs right here and not in some other place (in other words, heaven is not necessarily somewhere above us).

After the end of the world, all human beings who have ever lived will be resurrected and judged. Many Muslims believe that this resurrection is only spiritual and that humans will not be restored to their physical bodies. At judgment, they will stand face-to-face with God for the first time and will be expected to answer for their actions. Those completely free from sin will go directly to heaven. Others will have to spend time in hell to pay for their sins before they enter heaven to live eternally. Islam does not have a strong concept of eternal damnation in hell; people spend time there in accordance with the degree to which they have sinned. Certain special categories of sins (most notably *shirk*—the worshipping of other gods with Allah) warrant eternal damnation, though.

The Qur'an paints an extremely vivid picture of heaven as a garden with streams and fruit trees where humans will live a lavish and comfortable life. Many Muslims take this picture of heaven literally. Others see it as a metaphor for a state of spiritual bliss where the greatest reward will be living closely with God.

Pillars of Practice

Paralleling the Pillars of Faith are certain practices required of all pious Muslims: *shahada* (witnessing), *salah* (prayer), *zakah* (almsgiving), *sawm* (fasting), and *hajj* (pilgrimage). These constitute the fundamental ritual requirements of Islam. Even though they recognize the importance of these rituals, many Muslims do not observe all of them or they observe them partially. Islamic law also provides extensive guidelines on the circumstances under which an individual is not obligated to engage in ritual and on how an individual makes up for missed ritual obligations, thereby recognizing that certain circumstances (such as travel, illness, or pregnancy) make it difficult or impossible to participate in these rituals. It is important to make the formal intention to engage in a ritual before actually doing it, otherwise the ritual obligation has not been fulfilled. For example, Muslims are ritually obligated to give a percentage of their wealth in a form of charity called *zakah*. If an individual were to give away money without first making the conscious intention of fulfilling his or her *zakah* obligation, it would still be a good deed but would not count as *zakah*.

Shahada (Witnessing)

Shahada literally means "witnessing" and is a shorter form of the term *kalimat ash-shahada*, the statement of bearing witness that forms the creedal formula of Islam. The statement literally translates as "I bear witness that there is no god except Allah and I bear witness that Muhammad is the messenger of Allah!" Some people recite a slightly different version in which the second half of the statement is "I bear witness that Muhammad is his servant and his messenger."

This formula is often broken down into its components in order to show what the central beliefs of Islam are, especially the nature of the Islamic understanding of God. The whole formula is framed as an avowal or assertion: it is supposed to be a voluntary and conscious declaration of an individual's beliefs. The first half of the formula is an avowal of absolute, pure monotheism. It begins with a complete denial of the existence of any gods whatsoever ("There is no god!"). After metaphorically wiping the altar of a person's faith clean of the existence of all false gods, through uttering "except Allah," the person then asserts his existence uniquely. "There is no god except Allah" is therefore a much more powerful statement of monotheistic faith than something simpler like, "There is a God." This half of the *shahada* is sometimes called the Negation and Affirmation, in recognition of the way in which it asserts monotheism.

Uttering the first half of the *shahada* makes the person a monotheist but not necessarily a Muslim; it is something that could be said just as faithfully by Christians or Jews. It is the second half of the formula ("Muhammad is the messenger of Allah") that distinguishes Muslims from other monotheists because belief in the finality of Muhammad's prophetic mission is what sets Muslims apart from followers of other religions.

The *shahada* encapsulates the essence of Islamic faith so perfectly that many people consider uttering and believing in this formula more fundamental to being a Muslim than the other Pillars of Practice. For this reason, it is often referred to as the foundation stone on which the Pillars of Faith and Pillars of Practice stand. It is the first thing that is whispered into a baby's ears when he or she is born, and it is the utterance that Muslims try to have on their lips at the moment of death. It is also the formula by which a person converts to Islam, such that many people believe that simply uttering the *shahada* makes a person a Muslim.

Quick Facts: Conversion to Islam

Muslims believe that Islam was sent as the final religion for humankind and that the teachings of Islam apply to all peoples living in all times. Therefore, those born Muslim and those converted to it are not viewed differently in Islamic thought, although modern converts sometimes experience special challenges due to sociocultural issues. Conversion to Islam is simple; in order to become a Muslim, all someone has to do is recite the testimony of *shahada* with sincerity: "I bear witness that there is no God except Allah and I bear witness that Muhammad is the messenger of Allah!" However, prospective Muslims are encouraged to study the faith before making the commitment to convert.

Salah (Prayer)

Sunni and Twelver Shi'a Muslims (forming the majority of Muslims), are ritually required to pray five times a day. This particular kind of prayer, called *salah* in Arabic and *namaz* in many other languages, is very formal and ritualistic and is not to be confused with the informal, private prayer that most Muslims engage in anytime they feel like asking God for something.

Salah prayers are performed just before daybreak; just after the sun has reached the highest point in the sky; in the middle of the afternoon; just after sunset; and after it has gotten dark. It is worth noting that although all the prayers are linked to the sun, none is performed precisely at the moment of a sun-related time (e.g., precisely at sunrise or sunset). This is to consciously disassociate Islam from any form of sun worship. Twelver Shi'a followers believe that the midday prayers can be combined with others so that an individual only has to pray three times a day. This practice probably originates from a time when they were persecuted for their beliefs and therefore tried not to make any public displays of their faith, instead only praying when they were in the privacy of their homes or in the safe company of other Shi'a Muslims.

Muslims are not required to pray communally, although it is considered better to pray with other people when possible since this helps strengthen social bonds. A person can pray at home or anywhere else as long as the place is not unclean. Cleanliness is more a matter of ritual purity than of hygiene, although an obviously filthy place (such as a sewer or public restroom) is not appropriate for prayer. Ritually impure places are normally associated with death, be it human or animal. Not only would a slaughterhouse be considered impure for prayer, but some people would also consider a cemetery or even the tomb of a saint an impure place.

Prayer is preceded by a ritual of washing called *wudu* (or *wuzu*), which involves washing the hands, face, and feet in a prescribed way. Once again, this washing is a ritual purification and not a matter of hygiene. No soap is used, and when water is unavailable, the person can simply go through the motions of washing with dry hands. After entering such a state of ritual purity, the Muslim stands facing Mecca and makes the formal intention to pray. *Salah* prayers consist of prayer cycles made up of a set of verses recited in a series of standing, sitting, and kneeling positions. Each cycle is called a *rak'ah*, and the number of *rak'ah*s varies according to which of the daily prayers is being performed.

Believers have little latitude in what they say during the *salah*; the majority of verses or phrases are set, being derived from the Qur'an. There are certain points in each *rak'ah* cycle when individual Muslims can choose a selection from

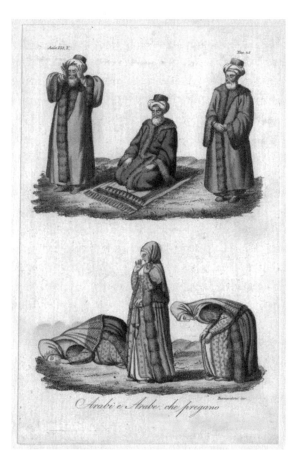

Arabi e Arabe che pregano

The illustration *Arabi e Arabe che pregano (Arabians Praying)* is from Giulio Ferrario's *Il costume antico e moderno, o, storia del governo, della milizia, della religione, delle arti, scienze ed usanze di tutti i popoli antichi e moderni* (Firenze: Batelli, 1823–1838). New York Public Library.

the Qur'an to recite, but they cannot choose anything else to incorporate into their prayer (e.g., a non-Qur'anic prayer or hymn). Furthermore, the *salah* prayers are always performed in Arabic, even by those Muslims (the majority) who do not understand the language. As such, *salah* is not prayer in the sense of a personal conversation with God but rather a ritual obligation that must be fulfilled to reaffirm the believer's relationship with God. Although a substantial number of Muslims offer the *salah* prayer five times a day, others do not. They might pray once or twice a day, once a week, or only on major religious holidays.

Sawm (Fasting)

Muslims are supposed to fast during the month of Ramadan, the ninth month of the Islamic lunar calendar. The fast (*sawm*) lasts from before sunrise until after sunset for the entire month and consists of abstaining from eating, drinking, smoking, committing acts of violence, and engaging in sex. The believer is supposed to refrain from these things and also from thinking about them. Going hungry and thirsty and avoiding violent or sexual thoughts is supposed to teach self-awareness and also make Muslims more sympathetic toward those less fortunate, who have to go without food and water out of necessity, and also have to hide their anger and desire because they always live at the mercy of others.

Ramadan is the holiest month of the Islamic year, and fasting is one of the most social of Islamic rituals. In countries with an Islamic majority, the entire daily schedule changes during Ramadan to accommodate the fast. Most families wake up before sunrise to eat a substantial breakfast and to pray. The beginning of the fast is either announced by a siren blast or else by men who walk through the streets beating a drum. Restaurants either close completely during the day or are very discreet about serving customers.

In some conservative societies, it is illegal to eat or drink in public, and only certain restaurants are allowed to stay open in order to feed non-Muslims or travelers (these tend to be in major hotels or near airports, bus stations, and train stations). Many Muslims "open," or break, the fast in a simple way by drinking water and eating either some salt or a few dates, in imitation of the way Muhammad was believed to open his fasts. Supper tends to be more lavish than it would be at other times of the year. The entire month has a festive atmosphere combined with a great sense of piety. Children often insist on fasting because fasting is associated with growing up, and the first time parents allow a child to fast for a whole day or for the entire month is a major event in many Muslims' lives.

The end of Ramadan is marked by a major religious holiday. Its official name is Eid al-Fitr, and it is known by other names in different Muslim countries, either as the Lesser Festival or the Sweet Festival, since preparing and eating sweets is one of the major family activities at this time.

Zakah (Almsgiving)

The giving of charity is considered an extremely meritorious act in Islam. As with prayer, a particular kind of almsgiving is differentiated from others because it is done ritually. Known as *zakah* or *zakat*, it consists of giving a certain percentage of a believer's wealth in charity. The percentage given away varies by sect, ranging from 2.5 percent among Sunnis to 10 percent in some Shi'a groups. A great deal of variation exists in what forms of wealth and income are considered taxable for *zakah*, for example, whether or not income (as opposed to assets) is taxable, and how to calculate the tax for agricultural products.

In some modern societies, the government collects the *zakah* tax in the same way as other taxes. This tax income is then used exclusively for religious purposes or for social welfare, such as the building of hospitals or schools. In other societies, people are responsible for making the charitable contributions to causes of their choice. Some Muslims give the entire sum to their local mosque or to a respected religious leader who then puts it to good use. Others divide the money and give some to charities and the rest directly to needy individuals. Until recent times, it was very common for Muslims to use their *zakah* to financially support a needy person or entire family for their lifetimes. For example, a wealthy family might decide to use their *zakah* to support a family of destitute orphans, paying for their schooling and marriages, and eventually setting them up in businesses or professions of their own. Others might choose to endow a school or hospital and then pay for its expenses. Such uses of *zakah* have become less common in modern times, but they are not unheard of. In addition, Shi'a Muslims also give a charitable contribution called *khums*, or 20 percent of their excess income, to be used for charitable or religious works.

Hajj (Pilgrimage)

Hajj is the name of the pilgrimage to Mecca that all Muslims are required to undertake once in their lives if they have the means to do so. This pilgrimage is distinct from lesser pilgrimages made to other holy sites (such as Jerusalem) that do not fulfill the hajj obligation. The hajj must also be done at a specific time of year, from the seventh to the tenth of the last month of the Islamic calendar, which is named Zu'l-hijja ("month of the hajj") in recognition of the ritual's importance. If the pilgrimage to Mecca is carried out at some other time of year, it is called an *umra*; it is still a good deed but does not fulfill a Muslim's duty to perform the hajj.

For roughly 1,400 years, the hajj has replayed the pilgrimage to Mecca performed by Muhammad after the city had surrendered to the Muslims. Pilgrims enter a state of ritual purity and wear a special pilgrim's dress before arriving in Mecca. They begin by walking seven times around the Ka'ba, the focal point of Islamic faith. Besides being the focus of the hajj, the Ka'ba indicates the direction in which Muslims pray regardless of where in the world they may be.

After completing their circuits around the Ka'ba, the pilgrims run between two small hills named Safa and Marwa. This ritual recalls an episode in the life of Abraham and his family in which Abraham abandoned Hagar and her infant son Ishmael (Isma'il in Arabic) in the desert. When Ishmael cried out in thirst, Hagar ran seven times back and forth between Safa and Marwa looking for water. In the meantime, Ishmael is believed to have kicked his heels against the sand, miraculously causing a spring to appear. This spring, called Zamzam, is

The physician and pioneer in Arab photography, al-Sayyid 'Abd al-Ghaffār, photographed these Muslims worshipping at the shrines sacred to Islam in Mecca, Saudi Arabia. Library of Congress.

believed to possess spiritual powers, and pilgrims take water from it as religious souvenirs at the completion of the hajj.

After completing the rounds between the two hills, the hajj pilgrims go to two towns near Mecca to commemorate other events in Abraham's life. The last part of the hajj involves spending an afternoon in the plain of Arafat where Muhammad delivered what came to be called his Farewell Sermon. The hajj ends on the third day, when the pilgrims sacrifice sheep, goats, and occasionally camels in memory of Abraham's willingness to sacrifice his son and God's substitution of a ram in his stead. This sacrifice ends the hajj, and the pilgrims are free to wear regular clothes and wash normally again. Following the hajj, many Muslims make a side pilgrimage to visit the Prophet's tomb in Medina and, when political circumstances permit, to visit Jerusalem.

Before the advent of air travel and modern shipping, going on the hajj was an arduous task that required a great deal of preparation. The slowness of the journey and the dangers involved also meant that anyone going on hajj had to settle their affairs and make provisions for their families with the real possibility that they might never come back. For these reasons, the departure of the hajj caravans was a major event in all Islamic towns. The importance of the pilgrims' departure remains to this day, and in many Islamic countries the departure of a particular ship or airplane is designated as the official beginning of the hajj caravans and is bid a ceremonial farewell by high-ranking government officials.

In modern times, the number of pilgrims in one hajj can approach 2 million. It is a feat of organization to enable that many people to perform the same rituals in the same place in a three-day period. The Saudi Arabian government has invested large sums of money to create pedestrian highways, tunnels, and galleries to make the hajj work as smoothly as possible. Jeddah International Airport, which serves Mecca, becomes one of the busiest airports in the world during the days immediately before and after the hajj.

Jihad (Striving)

A minority of Muslims believe that the *shahada* is so fundamental to being a Muslim that it is qualitatively different from the other pillars and serves as a foundation on which the other pillars stand. To keep the number of pillars at five, they add jihad to the list, a concept that is little understood. The term "jihad" literally means "striving" and is a shortened version of a longer name that means "striving in the path of God." The concept covers all activities that either defend Islam or further its cause. As such, wars in which Muslims tried to bring new lands under Islam were known as jihad wars, and were understood and justified by Muslims in a way similar to how Christians understood the crusades. In modern times, any war that is viewed as a defense of a believer's own country or home is sometimes referred to as a jihad. This understanding is very similar to what is called a "just war" in Western society. In similar fashion, political extremists who believe their cause is just often refer to their guerilla or terrorist wars as jihad, even when the majority of their own society consider their acts of violence to be completely unjustified.

For the majority of Muslims, the designation of a war as a jihad follows similar patterns to those of a "just war" for many Christians. The government promoting war would be under tremendous pressure to present the war to its citizens as a conflict between good and evil, in which the citizens see themselves as fighting on the side of good. This presentation is necessary because most people are not willing to kill or die unless it is absolutely justified. Jihad theory

In this engraving from the late 1800s, J. D. Woodward depicts the interior of Jerusalem's Dome of the Rock shrine, including some of the inner circle of piers and columns and the fine wrought-iron screen.

allows a soldier to kill the enemy in a justifiable way; without it, he would be committing murder, which is a very grave sin in Islam. Similarly, someone who dies in the just cause of jihad dies a martyr's death, and is forgiven his or her sins. In recognition of this status, martyrs do not need to undergo the funerary rites of being bathed and clothed in the clean shroud required for other Muslims.

Islamic scholars often differentiate between an outer and an inner jihad. Outer jihad is in the visible service of Islam. It includes jihad warfare as well as other activities, such as engaging in written defenses of Islam, performing missionary activity, or simply furthering one's own education. This kind of jihad is called "jihad of the pen," as distinct from warfare, which is referred to as "jihad of the sword."

Inner jihad is the struggle all individuals go through against their own baser instincts, in the effort to better themselves. It is seen as much more difficult to do than engaging in outer jihads of the pen or sword. In recognition of this difficulty, the inner struggle is sometimes called the "greater jihad," and warfare is called the "lesser jihad."

Jihad is an excellent example of a collective rather than an individual duty. It is necessary for an Islamic society to engage in jihad when this is called for, but it is not required that each and every individual volunteer for military duty. If for some reason enough people are not volunteering, then military service becomes an individual responsibility and jihad an individual duty, since the society is failing in its collective duty.

Worth Debating

One of the most pressing issues facing the Middle East in the twenty-first century is the conflict between Jewish Israelis and the Arabs in and around Israel. Although the conflict primarily began with the formation of the State of Israel in 1948, it has far-reaching religious and historical roots. The Muslims who lived in Palestine before its transformation into Israel recognized the area as full of sacred sites. For instance, Muslims believe that the Dome of the Rock shrine in Jerusalem marks the spot from which Muhammad made a journey to heaven in 619 CE. On the other hand, Jews in the Middle East recognize the area as the birthplace of their religion and Jerusalem, the capital city chosen by King David (d. 962 BCE), as the home of the Israelites.

After years of conflict, how do you think these two groups can resolve their issues? What religious similarities and history might they share that could be used to build common ground? Should other countries try to encourage a peace agreement, or should these two groups work toward their own solution?

The Mosque and Prayer

rayer occupies a central place in Islamic ritual and in individual piety. As mentioned in the chapter "Teachings," Muslims are ritually obligated to pray five times every day at prescribed times and in a prescribed manner. These prayers can be carried out individually or in a group (the latter being preferable because praying with others reinforces social bonds within a community). They can also be offered at home or in any other place that is not impure in a ritual sense. As such, Muslims have no formal need for a temple or other religious building corresponding to the role that a church fulfills in Christianity. There is, however, a stress on the benefits of praying together with other Muslims, particularly for the midday prayer on Friday, which is ideally offered communally. For this reason, there is a practical need for spaces that would allow Muslims to gather for communal prayers, and the mosque has its origins in this need.

The English word "mosque" is derived through Spanish and Latin from the Arabic word *masjid*, which literally means a "place for bowing down in prayer." The mosque has very few essential features, a direct result of the simplicity of the Islamic prayer ritual. The necessary architectural elements of a mosque include some sort of boundary that marks where the mosque ends and the outside world begins, and a marker pointing out the correct direction of prayers, toward the Ka'ba. In actual fact, in light of the importance of the mosque in Islamic social life, most mosques are buildings rather than simple open spaces, and many of them are so beautiful that they are counted among the greatest artistic achievements of Muslim cultural expression. Such mosques often have a large main hall, with a courtyard on one side for accommodating worshippers on exceptionally busy days, such as major religious festivals. The courtyard also contains a fountain used to perform the ritual ablutions that are required before praying.

Un muezzin appelant du haut du minaret les fidèles à la prière (1879), by the French artist Jean-Léon Gérôme (1824–1904), depicts a muezzin in a minaret calling the faithful to prayer.

Usually at least one minaret, a tall tower with a balcony, is attached to the mosque. Before the invention of loudspeakers, someone would climb to the top of the minaret five times a day and make the call to prayer. In modern times, minarets have loudspeakers, and the person making the call to prayer simply stands in front of a microphone in the mosque. Larger mosques often have more than one minaret; there may be a minaret at each of the four corners of the mosque or there may be small minarets on the corners of the courtyard and large ones on the hall.

The hall of the mosque is often elaborately decorated: the floor may be covered with anything from simple straw mats to expensive Persian carpets, and the walls may be done in ceramic tiles, stucco, or carved wood. There is a religious aversion to the representation of human beings or animals in art, so the mosaics, stucco reliefs, tiles, or paintings on the walls of a mosque either depict abstract patterns of vines, curving arabesques, or geometric tesselations. The most striking decorative feature of many mosques is the Arabic calligraphy that adorns the inside (and sometimes even the outside). Calligraphy is one of the most highly developed arts in Islamic culture, in part because many Muslims feel that writing the words of God (i.e., the Qur'an) in beautiful ways is a meritorious act.

The master Ottoman calligrapher Muhammad Shafiq (d. 1879)
excelled in instructional pieces like this one, which is filled with
intricate arabesque floral designs typical of the late Ottoman
period. It uses the *naskhī* script, which harmoniously connects
Arabic letters. Yale University Library.

Most large mosques have a small alcove or niche called the *mihrab* to mark the *qibla*, or direction of prayer. The *mihrab* is often beautifully decorated, even in mosques that are otherwise very simple. Mosques often also contain a *minbar*, or pulpit, which the leader of the prayers, or imam, uses to deliver the sermon. (This imam should not to be confused with the Shi'a imam, who is the political and spiritual leader of the entire community appointed by God.) *Minbars* can be fixed or movable; they are frequently intricately carved works of art. Some very large, imperial mosques also contain a raised platform or mezzanine where the king and his entourage could pray. (The platform was believed to provide protection from would-be assassins.) Other mosques have galleries or separate sections where women can pray, since men and women do not pray together in Sunni and Twelver Shi'a Islam. Beyond the features mentioned above, mosques contain no furniture or altars.

Even though the primary function of a mosque is to hold worshippers while they pray, mosques have been used since the time of Muhammad for many other purposes. Often they function as classrooms for formal and informal teaching. They are also used as a gathering or resting place for people to escape the hustle and bustle of city streets or as a cool refuge from the heat of the day. In many smaller towns, the mosque is the only large building, so it is used for many different kinds of community meetings in the same way a church is used. Mosques also occasionally provide a safe place to sleep for travelers who have no other place to go. Before the widespread availability of radio and television, the mosque was also the place to go for news, and many people attended the Friday sermon simply to get information on the political climate of the day.

Topics for Further Study

Architecture

Art—South Asia

Art—West Asia

Language

Quick Facts: Calligraphy

*A*s Islam spread west across North Africa to southern Spain, and east across Persia, the art of calligraphy began to develop as a means to proclaim the unity and victory of the Islamic faith. As the religion was introduced to other civilizations, Arabic became the instrument for differentiating Muslim places and objects from those of other cultures. Calligraphy developed as a way to decorate holy places and mundane articles, everything from mosques and palaces, to clothes and rugs, to decorative and utilitarian objects. Inscriptions from the Qur'an that were applied to a building or a fountain imbued the ordinary with the presence of the divine. During the period of Islamic expansion, from the seventh to the tenth centuries CE, enormous cultural and linguistic blendings and transformations occurred, resulting in the flowering of art, architecture, literature, and science. Even the Farsi and Turkish languages were transliterated into Arabized scripts, making universal the calligraphic styles that began in Arabia.

Arabic calligraphy soon became a form of ornamentation unique to the Muslim world. *Kufic* script, with its angular geometry and bold relief, can be chiseled into stone with a hammer. It has an imposing, architectural presence and became important for use on buildings. Geometrical instruments were created to apply *Kufic* inscriptions to massive structures. A highly ornamented variation of *Kufic* script was used for distinctive borders. It was also used in illuminated manuscripts of the Qur'an.

Thulth, or *thuluth*, script lends itself to other kinds of designs on manuscripts and decrees. Intertwining letters form an integrated design, creating suitable images for monograms and seals. The Ottoman Turks, like the Persians, used an Arabized alphabet to preserve their own linguistic traditions within the mold of the Qur'an's language. The Ottomans also developed the royal *diwani* script and created magnificent *tughras*, or seals, containing the name of each Ottoman sultan. *Tughras* were used instead of royal likenesses on coins, in deference to the Islamic proscription of depicting human images.

Arabic language united the many peoples who were enfolded into the Islamic empires and became the lingua franca of the Middle East. Islamic civilization incorporated Sasanid Persians, Byzantine Syrians, Hellenized Jews, Turks, Mongols, Afghanis, Berbers, and countless other peoples, and Arabic was the language used for cross-cultural communication. By blending Arabic with the architectural and artistic traditions of the conquered territories, Islamic civilization gave rise to a synthesizing aesthetic that enabled non-Muslims to identify with and participate in its cultural and commercial life. By the eighth century CE, Arabic would become a universal language of science, diplomacy, and culture, and it would remain so until the twelfth century. Arabic was the singular element that bonded the many into the whole.

Islamic Rites

*I*slamic societies the world over practice a number of rites to mark each individual's path through life, from birth to death. Most rites differ markedly in their details from one society to the next, and many, especially customs relating to marriage and childbirth, often bear little resemblance across cultures. Certain turning points in human life, however, are particularly emphasized as Islamic religious events by all Islamic societies and, at some basic level, are observed in similar ways. Three of these lifecycle rites are the circumcision of male children, marriage, and death and funeral customs.

Circumcision

Male circumcision is not mentioned in the Qur'an, but the practice is believed to be essential in all Islamic societies. It is mentioned in the hadith traditions as a custom practiced by all prophets before Muhammad and particularly by Abraham. This connection with the prophets of the Hebrew Bible suggests a connection between the Islamic practice of circumcision and its status in Judaism as a symbol of God's covenant with the people of Israel. Muslims also believe in a covenant between God and all human beings, but the Qur'an makes no connection between the covenant and the practice of circumcision.

Male children can be circumcised anytime from early infancy until the onset of puberty, depending on the culture they belong to and their parents' social class. For many urban families, the rite is performed on an infant in a hospital or clinic and is accompanied by little fanfare. For others, it occurs as part of a major ceremony and is a rite of passage remembered by the boy on whom it is performed. This is particularly true in Malaysia and Turkey, where circumcision usually occurs around the age of thirteen. The boy is dressed as a prince and, depending on the financial means of the family, a large feast follows the circumcision ceremony, at which time the boy receives many gifts. In these societies, the circumcision serves as a puberty rite that marks a boy's passage into adulthood. The public nature of the ceremony allows him to show his bravery and honor; following this ceremony, he is considered a full member of Islamic society and is expected to pray and fast like an adult.

The practice of female circumcision is unheard of in most Islamic societies, but it is practiced on girls in some Islamic societies, particularly in Africa. There is considerable variation in what precisely is involved in female circumcision; it can involve anything from a purely ritualistic scarring of the clitoral hood to the complete removal of the outer labia. In societies where it is commonly practiced, such as Egypt, where the rite is also found among Coptic Christians, critics vocally oppose it and refer to it as "female genital mutilation." The Egyptian government has banned the ritual, but it is so deeply ingrained in the society (where it has probably existed from the time of the pharaohs) that many families continue the practice in relative secret. Unlike male circumcision, which is frequently a public and festive event, female circumcision tends to be a quiet, family affair and is normally performed by midwives rather than the professionals or semiprofessionals who perform male circumcision.

Marriage

The majority of Muslims regard marriage as one of the basic components of Muslim social life. Although it is not explicitly listed as a religious duty, many people consider it as such and view a celibate or monastic life as somehow inferior and incomplete. Their justification lies in the frequent references to marriage in the Qur'an as well as in the custom of the Prophet Muhammad, who was married. Some believe he made strong statements in favor of marriage, such as that there should be no celibacy in Islam and that when people marry, they fulfill half their religious obligations.

The Qur'an contains extensive rules concerning who an individual is permitted to marry, what constitutes the rights and duties of a husband and wife, and ownership of property. Details that are not found in the Qur'an are filled in from the *sunna* of the Prophet and the living customs of each society.

Legal Status of Women

The revelation of the Qur'an to Muhammad occurred in the context of an extremely patriarchal society where almost all economic and social power rested with men. The Islamic laws concerning marriage and the status of women set down in the Qur'an explicitly listed many new rights that women could demand of the men in their society. Many of these rules may seem archaic or unfair when

---

Quick Facts: Why Did Muhammad Have Multiple Wives?

In the seventh century CE on the Arabian Peninsula, men commonly married more than one wife, especially since the frequent bloodshed left many women widowed at an early age. Muhammad never remarried while his significantly older first wife, Khadija, was alive. However, after the advent of Islam, he married up to eleven other women to cement political ties with various ethnic groups and to provide social support, as most of his wives were widows without livelihoods. None of the children of these later wives survived infancy. Despite the challenges of having such a large household, the hadith, or narrative record, indicates that the wives were treated fairly and justly with equal concern for their needs.

---

viewed from the perspective of modern Western society, but they constituted important reforms in the legal status of women.

According to Sunni Islamic law, a man can marry either a Muslim woman or one who belongs to another monotheistic religion. A woman, on the other hand, can only marry a Muslim man. This is because, in the Islamic legal view, the primary purpose for getting married is to provide a proper environment for raising children, and children are expected to follow the religion of their father. If the children's mother were a non-Muslim, the children would still be brought up as Muslims if their father were Muslim, but if their father were a non-Muslim, the children would be lost to the Islamic community. Shi'a law is even stricter on this issue and does not permit a Shi'a man to marry a non-Muslim woman. This, no doubt, derives from Shi'ism's status as a minority sect and their justifiable fear that too much intermarriage would dilute their identity and cause them to disappear.

Multiple Wives

Islamic law permits a man to marry up to four wives at one time. It encourages him to treat each wife equally, while at the same time it states that this is impossible to do. Those Muslims who are opposed to polygyny have seen these verses

Khadija (c. 554–619 CE)

Muhammad's first wife and the first convert to Islam, Khadija was a wealthy widow in the city of Mecca who had hired Muhammad to be her business manager. She was so impressed by his honesty and character that she asked him to marry her; Khadija was forty years old and Muhammad was twenty-five. Muhammad and Khadija lived a relatively quiet life until her death fifteen years later. They had six children: two boys, 'Abd Allah and al-Qasim, died in infancy; their four daughters grew up to be important members of the early Islamic community: Fātima, Ruqayya, Umm Kulthum, and Zaynab. These four daughters were the only children from Muhammad's marriages to survive into adulthood.

When Muhammad experienced his first revelation, he was terrified and went to Khadija for comfort, asking her to cover him with a cloak. Muhammad was scared and confused, and for a while after this first supernatural event, he refused to return to his cave to meditate. Khadija convinced him to return. She helped him make sense of the experiences he was undergoing, and when he finally understood his role as a prophet who was to invite people to the religion of Islam, Khadija became his first convert. Muhammad was extremely fond of Khadija throughout his life. He did not marry anyone else while Khadija was alive, and he reacted angrily when one of his later wives spoke ill of Khadija out of jealousy over his outright affection and admiration for his departed first wife.

of the Qur'an as an implicit forbidding of the practice. Some critics believe that polygyny was only permitted as a temporary measure because pre-Islamic Arab men were used to having many wives and would not accept a sudden change in their marriage customs.

The Qur'an also provides detailed rules about which relatives are permitted to marry each other. In practical terms, the only difference with common Western practices is that it is permissible for first cousins to marry. In many tradi-

Quick Facts: Why Do Muslim Women Wear the Hijab?

In Islam, both men and women are expected to dress modestly. According to some Muslim understandings, after reaching physical maturity girls are expected to cover their entire bodies except for their faces, hands, and feet when they are in front of men who are not their close blood relatives or husbands; some interpretations of Islamic law require them to cover their faces and feet as well. This type of modest dress is called the *hijab*, and it includes a covering for the hair, most often a head scarf. No one style or color of clothing is required, and Muslim cultures have developed a variety of traditional clothing that meets the requirements of the *hijab*. The *hijab* is meant to promote chaste interactions between men and women, to discourage extramarital relationships, and to strengthen the marital bond. In modern times, many Muslim women have also looked to the *hijab* as a form of liberation that allows them to participate actively in society while being judged for their humanity instead of their sexuality.

tional Muslim societies, this is the preferred form of marriage because it reinforces family bonds and ensures that property remains within the extended family.

Marriage as Legal Contract

In its barest essence, the Islamic institution of marriage is a legal, contractual arrangement that provides a materially secure environment for children to grow up in and a socially acceptable outlet for sexual desire. The letter of the law sees marriage as nothing more than this and therefore concentrates on the details of entering into the contract, making provisions for breaking it in the event of divorce. Every Islamic culture, however, attaches great importance to the marriage ceremony and buries the legal parts of the ceremony in an ornate series of celebrations. Even though the people engaging in these marriage ceremonies would find it difficult to separate the religious from the cultural part, these marriage customs are primarily cultural. A Syrian Muslim ceremony is very similar

The Tajik Muslims of Turkistan are known for elaborate wedding rituals that can last an entire week. Library of Congress.

to a Syrian Christian one, just as an Indian Muslim wedding shares a great deal with a Hindu one.

The legal center of the Islamic marriage ceremony involves the signing and witnessing of the marriage contract. This contract can be signed either by the bride and groom or by their guardians. An important aspect of the contract is the fixing of a "bride price." This is a sum of money given by the groom to the bride that becomes her personal wealth. In some cultures, the bride price can be extremely high; most of it is not given to the bride at the beginning of the marriage but is promised to her in the event that the husband divorces the wife. In this way, it serves as a strong disincentive for men to initiate divorce. In other cultures, the bride price is considered little more than a formality or quaint custom and is a nominal amount. Nevertheless, the fact that it persists shows its central place in the Islamic marriage contract.

Divorce

The Islamic laws concerning marriage allow for the possibility of divorce. It is legally easier for a husband to divorce his wife than the other way around. Even so, there are clear provisions through which a woman can sue for divorce from her husband over things like abuse, neglect, or abandonment. Most Muslim societies continue to be socially conservative and family oriented, however, and even though divorce is legally permissible, there is enormous social pressure not to get divorced. There is a very famous saying attributed to the Prophet Muhammad that of all the things allowed by God, the most distasteful is divorce.

Death

Muslims view death as the culmination of life, at which time human beings return to God and answer for their actions in this world. Just as it is viewed in most religions, death is viewed by Muslims as a passage from one sort of life to the next, and it serves as a major life rite.

Ideally, Muslims should die facing the direction of the Ka'ba in Mecca and with the Islamic profession of faith, "There is no god but Allah and Muhammad is the messenger of Allah," on their tongues. If dying people cannot do this on their own, then attending family members often help them face the correct direction and repeat the profession of faith so that it is the last thing they hear as they pass on. In many societies, people also recite the thirty-sixth chapter of the Qur'an, titled "Ya-Sin," which has many powerful verses dealing with the subject of death.

People are supposed to be buried within a day of their death. People who die in the morning should be buried before nightfall; if death occurs in the evening, the dead should be buried the next morning. In actual practice, burials are often delayed by several days when, for example, an individual dies away from home and has to be brought back for burial.

The body is ritually bathed after death, a task that is traditionally performed by family members who belong to the same sex as the deceased. This washing follows the same fashion as the ritual ablutions performed before prayer, except that the body is washed an odd number of times (usually three) using soap and water that is sometimes perfumed. There is no tradition among Muslims of embalming, dressing, or adorning the body. The washed body sometimes has a touch of perfume dabbed on various parts; sometimes cotton is placed on the major orifices and the unclothed body is wrapped in a white cotton shroud that covers it from head to toe. Coffins are not normally used, and when they are, they are made of very simple materials.

The only acceptable way to dispose of a body according to most Muslims is through burial under ground (cremation or entombing an embalmed body above ground are not permitted). The grave is approximately 5 feet deep with an alcove carved out at the bottom (such that the grave has an L-shaped cross-section). The body is placed in this alcove resting on its right side with the head facing Mecca. The alcove is then closed in (sometimes with unfired clay bricks), and then the grave is filled in. Strict interpretations of Islamic law do not allow the construction of permanent graves; instead, they require graves to be simple mounds of dirt with perhaps a simple gravestone marking the site.

In practice, there is a long-standing tradition in all Islamic regions of making elaborate graves, and some of the innumerable mausoleums of saints and aristocrats are masterpieces of architecture. The Taj Mahal in Agra, India, is an example of such a tomb, as is the Mamluk necropolis in Cairo, Egypt. In some places, entire cities have grown around the tomb of a highly respected religious person, such as the cities of Karbala in Iraq, Mashhad in Iran, and Mazār-e Sharīf in Afghanistan.

Funerals

Islamic burial is traditionally accompanied by a simple funeral service. This consists of the carrying of the funeral bier to the cemetery and the offering of funeral prayers. The bier (often a simple cot with the corpse on it, shrouded in a white or green sheet) is carried by four men at a time. Men in the funeral procession continuously trade places, taking turns carrying the bier. Joining in a funeral procession is considered a collective duty; if there are not enough people accompanying the body to the cemetery, individual Muslims are duty bound to join in; if there are enough people then they are not.

The funeral prayer is a variation on the *salah*, an Islamic ritual prayer; so the funeral prayer is a kind of *salah*. The major difference is that the funeral ritual includes the recitation of several prayers for the deceased, asking for the dead person to be guided and forgiven in the afterlife. An interesting variation in Islamic rites concerning death and burial involves the treatment of children and martyrs. Since small children are not believed to be accountable for their actions, the funeral prayer does not include asking for forgiveness on their behalf. Similarly, martyrs are believed to be absolved of all sins, so forgiveness of their sins is not requested either.

Islamic societies differ greatly in how they perform funeral rites, both in terms of how the body is taken to the cemetery and how mourning is performed. In many societies, there are set days after the burial (especially the fortieth day) when special rituals are performed to remember the deceased. These normally involve the distribution of food or money among the needy and the gathering of mourners to read the Qur'an.

Topics for Further Study
Clothing and Costume
Initiation and Rites of Passage
Law, Sacred
Matriarchy and Patriarchy

Islamic Holidays

All Islamic religious holidays follow the Islamic lunar calendar. Called the Hijri calendar in recognition of Muhammad's Hijra, or migration, from Mecca to Medina, it follows the lunar year, which is about eleven days shorter than the solar one. This means that Islamic holidays appear to move backward through the year, and holidays that are in the middle of summer one year are in the middle of winter a decade later. This prevents Islamic holidays from developing a seasonal character the way Catholic and Jewish holidays have.

Some holidays are official or central to the religion and are observed by all Muslims. But if the holidays belong to a particular sect, then they may be observed only by members of that sect. Others, such as festivals of saints, are specific to a particular place. In addition to these holidays, Muslims have seasonal holidays that tend to be less religious in character. The best-known of these is the celebration of the Persian New Year, or Nowruz. It coincides with the spring (vernal) equinox and is widely celebrated in Iran and its surrounding countries.

Eid al-Fitr (at the end of Ramadan)

Eid al-Fitr ("Festival of Breaking the Fast") is celebrated on the first of Shawwal, the tenth month of the Islamic year. This holiday commemorates the end of the month-long fasting during Ramadan, when adult Muslims are supposed to abstain from eating and drinking from before sunrise until after sunset. The month of Ramadan places stress on the fasting individuals as well as the general society, because the change in the eating schedule and the increase in the amount of time spent in prayer disrupts the rhythms of everyday life. (Some argue that this is exactly what it is meant to do.) The festival of Eid al-Fitr brings the changed rhythms of Ramadan to an end so that life can return to normal after the holiday.

In many ways, Eid al-Fitr is the opposite of Ramadan. It is marked by a midmorning communal prayer that is so well attended in many towns that the main mosques cannot hold all the worshippers and prayer services have to be held in public places such as fairgrounds and large squares. Whereas during the month of Ramadan fasting Muslims eat two large meals a day, on Eid al-Fitr they normally do not eat regular meals but snack for the entire day. The atmosphere of this holiday is festive and celebratory: schools and offices are closed for two days in most countries, and for longer in others; those who can afford new clothes wear them; and children receive gifts from older relatives, most often money.

Eid al-Adha (Hajj)

This is the holiest of Islamic holidays and marks the culmination of the hajj, the pilgrimage to Mecca that every Muslim is supposed to make once if he or she has the means to. This holiday falls on the tenth of the final month of the Islamic calendar, called Dhu.

Dhu'l-Hijja (or Zu'l-Hijja, "Month of the Hajj")

The main feature of this holiday is the sacrifice of animals, which commemorates the willingness of Abraham to sacrifice his son for the sake of God. In the Islamic version of this story, which is also found in the Bible, God asks Abraham to show his devotion by sacrificing the thing dearest to his heart. Abraham feels that this is his son Ishmael and tells Ishmael what has been asked of him. Ishmael agrees without hesitation to be the sacrificial victim. Abraham cannot bear to watch himself kill his own son, so he puts on a blindfold and cuts Ishmael's throat. When he takes off the blindfold, Abraham is astonished to see Ishmael standing unharmed beside him and a sacrificed ram at his feet, which God substituted in place of Ishmael. Muslims who have the financial means are expected to sacrifice rams to commemorate this event. In some cultures, people use other domesticated animals, such as goats, cattle, or camels. The main requirement is that the animal be a healthy adult male.

The flesh of the animal is divided among family, neighbors, and the poor. Since every pilgrim at the hajj sacrifices an animal, the amount of meat at Mecca at this time far exceeds the ability of people to consume it. In order to prevent waste, this meat is canned and relief organizations use it throughout the year. Many Muslims who live as minorities in western Europe or the United States find it difficult to fulfill their obligation to sacrifice an animal. Several international relief organizations will perform the sacrifice for a fee and distribute the meat to the needy in a country of the person's choice.

Muharram

Muharram is the name of the first month of the Islamic calendar. It has become synonymous with the name of a mourning ritual practiced by members of the Twelver Shi'a sect to commemorate the martyrdom of Muhammad's cousin 'Ali and, more importantly, 'Ali's son and Muhammad's grandson Husayn, which is celebrated on Ashura, the tenth day of the month.

Over the first ten days of the month, people engage in many activities to commemorate the martyrdom of Husayn and most of his immediate family. Professional storytellers relate colorful and heartrending versions of the tale every night in front of tearful audiences, some of whom beat themselves as a gesture

'Ali ibn Abi Talib (c. 600–661 CE)

Muhammad's first cousin, 'Ali ibn Abi Talib, was the son of the uncle who raised Muhammad after he was orphaned. When Muhammad was an adult, 'Ali came to live with him and later married Muhammad and Khadija's daughter Fatima, with whom he had four children: Hasan, Husayn, Zaynab, and Umm Kalthum. 'Ali is considered the second convert to Islam, after Khadija, and the first male convert.

'Ali was one of Muhammad's closest male companions, and he is among the most valiant warriors to fight in the service of Islam, receiving the title "Lion of God." Occasionally, when Muhammad was away on a journey, he would leave 'Ali in charge of the *ummah*, or community. Because of these roles, a substantial minority of Muslims believes that 'Ali should have been appointed leader of the Islamic community after Muhammad's death. Over time, the Shi'a religious sect emerged, believing that there is a supernatural reason for why 'Ali is more qualified than any of Muhammad's other companions to lead the *ummah*. But even Sunni Muslims, who do not agree with the Shi'a position, hold 'Ali in high regard. Many Sufis, most of whom are Sunni, consider 'Ali to be the first Sufi and believe their form of Islam derives from him.

of mourning. There are also "passion plays," called *ta'ziyah*s, which act out the trials and martyrdom of Husayn and his family.

The most distinguishing ritual performed during the month of Muharram is the mourning procession, also called a *ta'ziyah*. The procession has a few central objects: lights leading the procession, a float representing the coffin of Husayn, some sort of container for his weaponry, and a horse to stand in place of his horse. Frequently another float or wagon carries little children dressed in traditional Arab clothes who represent those members of Husayn's family taken prisoner after his martyrdom. The procession is accompanied by mourners, who engage in some form of ritual mourning, including cutting themselves with knives and razor blades. The bloodiest and most dramatic processions take place among the Shi'a believers of Pakistan and Lebanon. In Pakistan, the mourning activity tends to be relatively disorganized and, usually, semiprofessional "mourners" use knife blades bunched together at the end of chains to cut themselves on the shoulders and back. The Lebanese ritual is more organized: Mourners come as part of neighborhood religious organizations, and the most dramatic mourners cut themselves on the forehead with a razor blade or knife, and then repeatedly slap the wound to prevent it from clotting. They also dress in white sheets so that the blood stands out.

Shi'a clergy in all societies frown upon these violent mourning rituals and actively discourage the population from engaging in them. But these rituals have such a deep-seated importance to many Twelver Shi'a believers that they ignore the warnings of their clergy and continue to engage in these potentially dangerous practices.

Popular Holidays

In addition to the major religious holidays, several others holidays are also celebrated in varying ways in Muslim societies. These include the birthday of the Prophet, celebrated on the twelfth of Rabi' al-awwal, the third month; the Night of Ascension (Laylat al-Mi'raj or Shab-e Mi'raj on the twenty-seventh of Rajab, the seventh month); and the Night of Power (Laylat al-Qadr, on the night between the twenty-sixth and twenty-seventh of Ramadan), which commemorates the first revelation of the Qur'an to Muhammad. Many Muslims stay awake in prayer for this entire night, believing that requests made on this night will by granted by God.

Shrine Cults

Since the earliest times, shrine cults have provided a place for interreligious encounter and exchange, even for the sharing of faith, between many everyday Jewish, Christian, and Muslim peoples in the Middle East. The peoples of these three faiths share many of the same historical religious figures, whose burial places (i.e., shrines) they visit together. They are often found praying and "worshipping" side by side at each other's shrines, looking to the saints found in the other monotheistic faith traditions for help and hope in their daily lives.

In many ways, Islamic religion and devotion within the former Soviet Union (1922–1991) was saved by women followers of the shrine cults. Because of the Soviet repression of religion, many mosques were closed (as were Russian Orthodox churches and other places of worship), and attendance was severely restricted, if not prohibited at times. When attendance was permitted, it was primarily for men. But few men took advantage of the opportunity because it would raise suspicions about their commitment to Soviet ideology, which held, in accordance with the teachings of the philosopher Karl Marx, that "religion was the opium of the masses." Thus, they might be harassed by officials or other community members or treated as outcasts if they attended religious services. Amid this repressive atmosphere, however, little attention was paid to the Muslim religious devotion taking place at the shrines, especially at the many small ones found in and around cemeteries throughout villages and communities. Women in particular gathered at these shrines to pray for God's help and protection for their families and themselves and to seek healing, success, prosperity, and other blessings through the saints enshrined in those places. The women took their children with them because they had to care for them, and thus passed on their faith to their children, preserving it through the generations who lived under Soviet oppression until religious freedom was gained with the collapse of the Soviet Union.

Islamic Saints

Despite the fact that most strict interpretations of Islam reject the existence of saints or any other class of human beings having the power to intercede with God on behalf of ordinary Muslims, the majority of Muslims believe in and venerate saints in a variety of ways. There are two main types of saints, the first of which is made up of members of Muhammad's family. Their shrines are pilgrimage sites visited by Shi'a followers as well as Sunnis who hold the family of Muhammad in high regard even though they do not give them the religious importance that the Shi'a followers do.

The second type consists of important Sufi figures whose shrines are famous at a local or regional level as a place where prayers have a good chance of being answered. An example of a local saint is Telli Baba ("Father Tinsel"), whose shrine north of Istanbul, Turkey, is visited by women who are looking for a husband. The strange name of the shrine derives from the fact that the tomb is covered in pieces of tinsel that Turkish brides wear as part of their wedding celebrations. Visitors take a piece of tinsel from the tomb, and when their wish has been granted (they get married), they return with an offering of money and a handful of their tinsel, which is added to the tomb.

There are innumerable local shrines of this type in Muslim regions that are visited by people asking for some need to be fulfilled. Other Sufi shrines have an international importance and are visited by millions of people, particularly on festivals that commemorate the birth or death of the saint. These include the shrine of Sayyida Nafisa in Cairo, Abd al-Qādir al-Jīlānī in Baghdad, and Mu'inuddin Chishti in Ajmer, a city in northwestern India.

Sayyida Nafisa was the great-granddaughter of Hasan, the elder son of 'Alī and Fātima, daughter of the Prophet. She lived the latter part of her life in Egypt, where she became famous as a saint with miraculous powers. Her shrine and mosque complex are the center of a major festival and receive many visitors and petitioners throughout the year. Abd al-Qādir al-Jīlānī was the founder of the Qadiriyya Sufi order, the most widely distributed order. Mu'inuddin Chishti brought the Chishti Sufi order to India, and it is extremely popular in India, Pakistan, Afghanistan, and Bangladesh, in part because many musicians and artists belong to it.

Islamic Law (Sharia)

Many pious Muslims believe that one of the most remarkable and valuable features of their religion is the comprehensive and dynamic nature of its legal system. Islamic religious law is an elaborate and vigorous system that has been evolving from the time of Muhammad until the present and continues to be taken seriously by many Muslims who use its rules and values as guiding principles in their lives. This system of law is called the sharia, which literally means "path to water." This meaning shows how Muslims see the sharia as something essential to life and as an obvious path, because in a desert, nothing is more obvious to the residents as the path to a reliable source of water.

Sources of Law

Islamic law is believed to be the collected prescriptions for the running of the universe, as dictated by God. This law is revealed by God in the Qur'an, which provides some clear rules on issues as diverse as how to perform acts of worship, what not to eat, and how to distribute inheritance property. The Qur'an, however, does not provide clear rules for all of the innumerable situations encountered in the course of human life, whether during modern times or during Muhammad's time. In his time, the *ummah* did not see this as a problem because it had the living example of the Prophet to follow.

The generations living immediately after Muhammad's death also did not have any problem with the fact that the Qur'an does not provide a comprehensive list of laws, because the memory of Muhammad was very much alive in the *ummah*, and people felt they had a good idea of what Muhammad would have done in any given situation. But as generations passed, and

99

Worth Debating

In 2010, Indonesia was ranked as the country with the world's largest Muslim majority. Close to 90 percent of its inhabitants are Muslim. The country also celebrates the influence of Hinduism, found throughout its islands, and supports the national motto "Unity in Diversity." Indonesia maintains a modern approach to religion and politics through Islam-based political groups and a thriving democratic government. In fact, within the G-20, a group of countries committed to maintaining economic stability, Indonesia ranks third for best economic growth.

In sharp contrast to Indonesia is the Islamic country of Saudi Arabia. This country does not allow women to drive, segregation between the sexes is the norm, and police regularly punish citizens for violating religious law. The government is primarily a monarchy and operates under the Qur'an, which is the country's constitution.

Should an Islamic country use the Qur'an as its constitution or should religion and state be separate?

Duff, Mark. (2002, October 25.) Islam in Indonesia. *BBC News World Edition*. Retrieved April 14, 2010, from http://news.bbc.co.uk/2/hi/asia-pacific/2357121.stm

Indonesian president says Islam, democracy, modernization can develop together. *International Islamic News Agency*. Retrieved August 11, 2010, from http://www.iina.me/english/news.php?go=fullnews&newsid=195

the Islamic community spread to new cultures and faced new situations, it became more difficult to use Muhammad's practices, as they were remembered by the *ummah*, to guide all aspects of life. It therefore became necessary to create a system to develop laws to deal with new situations. This system is called *fiqh* and it has four principles called *usul al-fiqh* ("principles of jurisprudence").

The twelfth-century-CE Hanafi jurist Sirāj al-Dīn Muhammad ibn Muhammad 'Sajāwandī wrote a treatise on inheritance law called *The Shares According to Sirāj*; this edition was published in 1886 or 1887 in Lahore, now a city in Pakistan. Library of Congress.

Principles of Jurisprudence

The primary source of Islamic law is the Qur'an. Rules and precepts that are clearly stated in the Qur'an are not open to debate and must be accepted as is. By way of example, since the Qur'an explicitly forbids the eating of pork, Muslims who observe the *sharia* see no need to look for other sources of rules concerning whether or not they should eat pork.

If the Qur'an does not provide clear rules concerning a question of law, then followers look to the example of the Prophet: his *sunna* (the way Muhammad lived his life). This is preserved as "living *sunna*" in the practices of a virtuous Islamic community, and as "recorded *sunna*" in the anecdotes concerning Muhammad's actions, the hadith. The concept of *sunna* is complicated and open to interpretation, since the vast number of individual hadith accounts sometimes contradict each other. Furthermore, the concept of "living tradition" can cause conflict because not everyone agrees on which traditions of a society are in keeping with what Muhammad would have done and which are innovations. Since the ninth century CE, Muslim jurists have been deeply concerned about the need to come up with a scientific way of balancing the Qur'an and *sunna* and deriving laws from these sources that can be applied to new situations. This normally involves reasoning by analogy (the third principle of jurisprudence) and consensus of the community (the fourth).

Sunni Muslim jurists belong to four schools, which differ in whether they place more trust in the textual sources of the Qur'an and hadith or in the human ability to reason by analogy. These schools are called the Maliki, Hanbali, Hanafi, and Shafi'i. The Maliki school is traditionally strongest in North Africa and considers the living *sunna* of the *ummah* to be more reliable than human reason. The Hanbali school is strongest in Saudi Arabia; it has historically given a great deal of weight to the literal interpretation of written texts, so much that some Hanbali scholars insist that an unreliable hadith should be preferred over a strong example of reasoning by analogy. The Hanafi and Shafi'i schools together apply to the majority of Sunni Muslims and have a wide distribution. The Shafi'i school is more popular among the Arabs of the Middle East and Indonesia, and the Hanafi school is more accepted in South and Central Asia and Turkey. The Hanafi school has had a wider distribution since the sixteenth century, but before that the Shafi'i school was the most influential legal tradition in Islamic communities. Twelver Shi'a followers have one important legal school, which is named the Ja'fari school after the sixth imam, Ja'far as-Sādiq.

Quick Facts: Islamic Law and the Call to Prayer

The best way to explain how the principles of jurisprudence (*usul al-fiqh*) work is to use an example, such as whether it is permissible to use a loudspeaker to make the Islamic call to prayer. Of course, neither the Qur'an nor the hadith (narrative) has an explicit reference to loudspeakers (or any other electrical device). On the other hand, several places in the Qur'an encourage people to pray. Hadith accounts also state that Muhammad appointed a particular person to make the call to prayer because of his strong and attractive voice, and that this man used to stand on high ground to so that the call would carry further.

Reasoning by analogy, a legal scholar would argue that the Qur'an encourages prayer as an activity, and that the Prophet appointed a particular person to make the call to prayer precisely so that his voice would reach the widest possible audience. That this man also stood on high ground also indicates that the Prophet wanted the call to prayer to reach as far as possible. Since a loudspeaker in no way changes the call to prayer but only makes it louder, thereby allowing it to be heard by more people, Islamic law (sharia) should permit its use. If there were little or no objection to this legal opinion and several other judges arrived at a similar decision, there would be a consensus that using loudspeakers to make the call to prayer would be accepted by Islamic law (as, in fact, it has been accepted).

Many Muslim societies had developed specialized legal practitioners by the fourteenth century CE. A *faqih* is a scholar who specializes in the theoretical study and interpretation of Islamic law. A mufti is usually appointed by a ruler to answer people's questions about sharia.

Ahmad ibn Hanbal (780–855 CE)

Ahmad ibn Hanbal is among the most influential and respected Islamic legal scholars and theologians. The Hanbali school of law is named after him. He was also a very important scholar of hadith (narrative) traditions and the *Musnod ibn Hanbal*, one of the six respected collections of the hadith. Ibn Hanbal's main religious goal was to follow the example of the Prophet as closely as he could. He went as far as wearing his hair the way Muhammad was believed to and eating certain foods and avoiding others simply because Muhammad had liked or disliked them. His desire to imitate the Prophet was the motivation behind his decision to become a collector of the hadith, and it also formed the basis of his theories regarding the nature of Islamic law.

Ibn Hanbal refused to accept that human intellect was as reliable a source of law as prophetic tradition. This brought him into direct opposition with the theological position of the Mu'tazila, and he was persecuted for disagreeing with the accepted theology of the day. He was so popular among the people of Baghdad, however, that riots broke out and the caliph was forced to free him. A legend claims that while Ibn Hanbal was being flogged under the caliph's orders, his loincloth started to come undone. Ibn Hanbal, who had not asked God to save him from imprisonment or torture, asked God to prevent him from being humiliated by being naked in public. According to this legend, his loincloth miraculously redid itself and saved the pious Ibn Hanbal from public embarrassment.

The Hanafi and Shafi'i schools use the principle of reasoning by analogy to a much greater degree than do the Hanbali and Maliki schools. For this reason, many people see these schools as being better able to adapt to new circumstances. The process of using reasoning by analogy to come up with new laws for new circumstances is called *ijtihad*, and someone who is qualified to engage in this form of independent reasoning is called a *mujtahid*. Being a *mujtahid* is not normally a formal title given by a ruler or government but is bestowed by the local Islamic community to recognize a religious scholar's reputation for learning and good character.

Thought Experiment

Research a Muslim country and determine what laws a foreign visitor would have to follow. How would they differ from those a foreign visitor would follow in the United States? What problems might an American tourist have in conforming to sharia (Islamic law), even if only for a short time? What would you think about this situation if you were visiting the Muslim country?

Faqihs, Muftis, and Fatwas

By the fourteenth century, many Islamic regions had developed specializations within the practice of law with different titles for each one. The scholar who engaged in the theoretical study and interpretation of Islamic law was called a *faqih*. People with questions concerning the law would go to a mufti, who was normally appointed by the ruler for the specific purpose of answering questions concerning the sharia.

At times, the mufti was a highly respected *faqih* who became a mufti simply because he gained a reputation among the local populace as a good, reliable scholar. The mufti's answer to questions is called a fatwa, best translated as a legal opinion or decree. In theory, the mufti's opinion is binding on the person who posed the legal question. In practice, people frequently ignore the mufti's opinion if it displeases them, largely because there is no institution to enforce the decision. The office of a judge, that is, someone who presides over a court and has the power of the state and its police to enforce his opinions, is fulfilled by a *qadi*. *Qadi*s are government officials appointed by the rulers. This is why there have been many occasions when *qadi*s and *faqih*s have been at odds with each other; many *faqih*s consider government employment to be inappropriate for a scholar of law because there is too much temptation to compromise in matters of principle.

Challenges of the Modern Era

Excerpted from "Islam," by John O. Voll, in the Berkshire Encyclopedia of World History, 2nd Edition:

Although Islam was initially historically identified with Arabs, today only around 15 percent of the world's Muslims are Arabs, with the largest national communities of Muslims being in southern and southeastern Asia.

This powerful and expanding Islamic world had long interacted with western European and Christian-majority societies. These interactions entered a major new phase during the eighteenth century with the transformation of western European societies, especially through the Industrial Revolution, and the beginnings of European imperialist expansion. Throughout the Islamic world Europeans came to dominate Islamic lands, and Muslims responded in many ways. Muslims mounted major efforts to fight European expansion, as in the wars led by the emir (ruler) Abd al-Qadir in Algeria after the French invasion of 1830. Most military opposition failed.

Leaders in major Islamic countries introduced programs of reform to reshape their societies and states using Western models. Early reformers included Muhammad Ali in Egypt (reigned 1805–1849) and the Ottoman sultan Mahmud II (reigned 1808–1839), whose programs laid the foundations for the emergence of modern-style secular states. Later other reformers emphasized intellectual and religious dimensions. By the end of the nineteenth century efforts to create an effective synthesis of

Islam and modernity resulted in the movement of Islamic modernism. Major figures are Muhammad Abduh (1849–1905) and Jamal al-Din al-Afghani (1839–1897), whose ideas influenced groups as diverse as the Muhammadiyya movement established in Java in 1912 and intellectuals in India and North Africa. A different emphasis in reform is provided by more puritanical movements that seek a "return" to a more strict adherence to Islamic norms interpreted in a relatively literalist manner. This mode of reform has deep roots in Islamic history and can be seen in the premodern movement of Muhammad ibn Abd al-Wahhab (1703–1792), whose ideas have been an important part of modern Islamic revivalist movements.

The broad spectrum of responses to the challenges of modernity in the nineteenth century extended from the Westernizing programs of state reform to the explicitly Islamic modernists and fundamentalists. The work of all of these people set the framework for the developments of states and societies in the Muslim world during the twentieth century. By the end of the nineteenth century few groups could be considered purely non-modern (or, in the terminology of twentieth-century social scientists, "traditional"), since even the most conservative were interacting with the modernity of the time. That era was still largely defined by western European experiences, so that modernization tended to be viewed as a process of Europeanization or Westernization. But by the end of the nineteenth century, distinctive non-European modes of modernity were beginning to be visible, and the emergence of these different styles of modernity would play an important role in shaping the history of Muslim societies and thought in the twentieth century.

Twentieth-Century Modernity

Global Muslim communities experienced important transformations during the twentieth century. At the beginning of the century, most of the Muslim world was under direct or indirect European imperialist control, and the emerging political systems were primarily conceived as Western-style nation states. Explicitly Islamic movements and organizations were often viewed, even by "modern" Muslims, as anachronisms and obstacles to modernization. By the end of the twentieth century, however, virtually every Muslim majority society was politically independent, and classical European imperialism was an image from a seemingly distant past. An explicitly Islamic republic was created by a revolution that overthrew a Westernizing autocracy in Iran in 1979, and the new Islamic republic was sufficiently strong at the beginning of the twenty-first century to be viewed as a potential nuclear power and as an important major regional power. Muslims and Islamic movements became major influential agents in global affairs.

This transformation involved three broad historical phases, which can be defined in terms of the evolution of modernity itself during the twentieth century. In the era of domination by European imperial powers during the first half of the century, most new movements followed European-style patterns of political development. Resistance to European rule took the form of nationalist movements, and social and political reforms were generally secular in orientation. Modernity was defined in western European terms. The most successful of these movements was led by Mustafa Kemal Ataturk, who built a secular nationalist state in Turkey after the collapse of the Ottoman Empire in World War I.

In the middle of the century, following World War II, the second phase was shaped by the experience of newly-achieved political independence. Most Muslim states became politically independent, and various forms of secular and radical nationalism dominated the intellectual and political scene. Leaders such as Gamal Abd al-Nasir in Egypt and Ben Bella in Algeria incorporated Islamic themes into their radical nationalist programs, but these programs were not primarily Islamic in orientation or identification. By the 1960s, it appeared that the most important political developments and reform movements in the Muslim world represented radical programs of modernity that competed with older visions of modernity. Competing definitions of modernity—or multiple modernities—shaped Muslim policies and visions. An important culmination of this development was the Islamic Revolution in Iran in 1979, when radicalism was defined in explicitly Islamic terms, and the older more secular forms of radicalism became marginalized.

By the final quarter of the twentieth century, distinctively Islamic modernities were articulated as the bases for social visions and political programs. The new movements in the third era of twentieth-century Muslim history had some roots in earlier organizations that were modern in organization but more puritanical in terms of intellectual content. The most important of these groups are the Muslim Brotherhood, established in Egypt by Hasan al-Banna in 1928, and the Jamaat-i Islam, established in 1941 in India by Abu al-Ala Mawdudi.

In the final decades of the century, the major signal that the radical and the secularist nationalist movements had failed to bring the expected prosperity and freedom to Islamic peoples was the Iranian Revolution of 1979, which brought to power a regime dedicated to a full implementation of Islamic rules and norms. During the early 1980s many other movements with strongly defined Islamic goals and agendas came to prominence. These movements represent the emergence of what came to be called "political Islam" because the primary focus of the programs was the control of the state. Some movements, such as the Islamic Salvation Front in Algeria, contested elections, whereas others, such as the Mujahidin in Soviet-occupied Afghanistan, engaged in violent opposition defined in its terms as jihad. These movements of jihad became a significant part of the Islamic experience of the 1990s. In the context of globalization, militant global networks such as al-Qaeda represented an important part of Islamic interaction with the world. However, such movements remained only a small part of Islamic life and often were in conflict with the mainstream Islamic organizations and sentiments that reflected the views of the majority of Muslims.

Although the movements of political Islam attracted the most attention, other important trends also developed during the 1980s. Intellectuals gave increasing attention to the definition of the place of women in Islamic society, and by the beginning of the twenty-first century, an "Islamic feminism" had emerged. This feminism involved a reexamination of the Qur'an, noting the Qur'an's emphasis on the equality of all believers and then noting the influence of more patriarchal perspectives in the way that the Islamic tradition was historically defined. Similarly, some intellectuals have emphasized pluralistic dimensions of the Islamic worldview and tradition and have also drawn back from the emphasis on political activism as a means for imposing Islamic norms.

Some of the impetus for these developments has come from the emergence of minority Islamic communities in western Europe and North America as important parts of the broader Islamic world. In those regions issues of gender equality and religious pluralism have great importance for Islamic community life.

New Twenty-First Century Realities

The continuing significance of religion at the beginning of the twenty-first century confirms the development of forms of modernities that are different from the definitions of modernity popular during the nineteenth and much of the twentieth century. Contrary to the expectations of theories of modernization in those periods, modernization did not mean the inevitable nonreligious secularization of state and society. In the Muslim world, new movements develop that are not simply continuations of old-style movements from premodern times or even twentieth century modern movements in some slightly different form.

The new movements that get the most attention are the militant movements like al-Qaeda. These are clearly different from the early Sufi movements of resistance to European imperialist expansion in the nineteenth century, and from the activist radical nationalist movements of the twentieth century. Globalization and the new electronic media of communication transform the nature of organization and shape the way that the messages of the movements are framed.

The largest of the new movements are not, however, the terrorist organizations. Throughout the Muslim world, new popular preachers and teachers have millions of followers in many countries. Islamic television ministries like that built by the Egyptian Amr Khaled are reshaping the ways that many Muslims participate in the sense of belonging to a global community of believers. Analysts speak of "iMuslims" and "e-jihad" in ways that illustrate the new modernities of Muslims in the world of the twenty-first century. The long history of the flexible adaptations of the Islamic community and belief system to changing historic conditions suggests that new forms of Islamic institutions and perspectives will continue to be defined by believers.

$\mathcal{R}$esources

These resources were selected to give readers a religious and cultural overview of the history of Islamic thought and expression.

History

Armstrong, Karen. (2000). *Islam: A short history.* New York: Modern Library.

Armstrong, Karen. (2006). *Muhammad: A prophet for our time.* New York: Atlas Books/ HarperCollins.

Eaton, Richard Maxwell. (1990). *Islamic history as global history.* Washington, DC: American Historical Association.

Egger, Vernon O. (2004). *A history of the Muslim world to 1405: The making of a civilization.* Upper Saddle River, NJ: Pearson Prentice Hall.

Elias, Jamal J. (2003). *The pocket idiot's guide to Islam.* Indianapolis, IN: Alpha Books.

Elias, Jamal J. (2010). *Key themes for the study of Islam.* Oxford, U.K.: Oneworld.

Esposito, John L. (1998). *Islam: The straight path* (3rd ed.). New York: Oxford University Press.

Esposito, John L. (Ed.). (1999). *The Oxford history of Islam.* New York: Oxford University Press.

Knysh, Alexander D. (2000). *Islamic mysticism: A short history.* Leiden, The Netherlands: Brill.

Kurzman, Charles. (Ed.). (2002). *Modernist Islam, 1840–1940: A sourcebook.* New York: Oxford University Press.

Lapidus, Ira M. (2002). *A history of Islamic societies* (2nd ed.). Cambridge, U.K.: Cambridge University Press.

Lewis, Bernard. (2002). *The emergence of modern Turkey* (3rd ed.). New York: Oxford University Press.

McCarthy, Justin. (1997). *The Ottoman Turks: An introductory history to 1923.* London: Addison Wesley Longman.

Nasr, Seyyed Hossein. (2004). *The heart of Islam: Enduring values for humanity.* San Francisco: Harper San Francisco.

Peters, F. E. (Ed.). (1994). *A reader on classical Islam*. Princeton, NJ: Princeton University Press.

Sonn, Tamara. (2004). *A brief history of Islam*. Malden, MA: Blackwell Publishing.

Voll, John O. (2000). Islam as a special world system. *Journal of World History, 5,* 213–226.

Modern Islam

Ahmed, Akbar S. (1999). *Islam today: A short introduction to the Muslim world*. London: I. B. Tauris.

Cole, Juan Ricardo. (2009). *Engaging the Muslim world*. New York: Palgrave Macmillan.

Dallal, A. S. (1995). Ummah. In John L. Esposito (Ed.), *The Oxford encyclopedia of the modern Islamic world* (pp. 267–270). New York: Oxford University Press.

Egger, Vernon O. (2009). *A history of the Muslim world since 1260: The making of a global community*. Upper Saddle River, NJ: Pearson Prentice Hall.

Elias, Jamal J. (in press). *On wings of diesel: Trucks, identity and culture in Pakistan*. Oxford, U.K.: Oneworld.

Khan, Saad S. (2001). *Reasserting international Islam: A focus on the organization of the Islamic conference and other Islamic institutions*. Karachi, Pakistan: Oxford University Press.

Mandaville, Peter G. (2001). *Transnational Muslim politics: Reimagining the umma*. London: Routledge.

Ramadan, Tariq. (2004). *Western Muslims and the future of Islam*. Oxford, U.K.: Oxford University Press.

Schulze, Reinhard. (2000). *A modern history of the Islamic world*. New York: New York University Press.

Sheikh, Naveed S. (2003). *The new politics of Islam: Pan-Islamic foreign policy in a world of states*. London: RoutledgeCurzon.

Tausch, Arno, & Hermann, Peter. (Eds.) (2006). *The West, Europe and the Muslim world*. New York: Novinka.

Classical Islamic Works

Al-Abidin, Zain. (1988). *The Psalms of Islam* (William C. Chittick, Trans.). London: Muhammadi Trust of Great Britain and Northern Ireland. (Originally published in the eighth century)

Barlas, Asma. (2002). *"Believing women" in Islam: Unreading patriarchal interpretations of the Qur'an*. Austin: University of Texas Press.

Esack, Farid. (2002). *The Qur'an: A short introduction*. Oxford, U.K.: Oneworld.

Jalāl ad-Din ar-Rūmī. (2003). *Rumi: The book of love: Poems of ecstasy and longing* (Coleman Barks, Trans.). New York: HarperSanFrancisco.

Khayyam, Omar. (2009). *The rubaiyat of Omar Khayyam* (Edward FitzGerald, Trans.). Oxford, U.K.: Oxford University Press. (Originally published in the twelfth century)

Children's Fiction

Brown, Tricia. (2006). *Salaam: A Muslim American boy's story*. New York: Henry Holt.

Khan, Rukhsana. (2002). *Muslim child: Understanding Islam through stories and poems*. Morton Grove, IL: Albert Whitman.

Yusufali, Salma. (2004). *Elephants, attack!* Houston, TX: Miskhat Publishing.

Multimedia

Akkad, Moustapha. (Director). (2005). *The message: The story of Islam* (30th anniversary ed.) [Motion picture]. United States: Starz/sphe. (Originally released in 1976)

Broughton, Simon. (Director). (2008, September 30). *The Sufi soul: The mystic music of Islam* [Documentary].

Koppel, Ted. (Anchor). (1997, 18 April). The Hajj: One American's pilgrimage to Mecca. *ABCNews Nightline* [Television broadcast and DVD].

Neibaur, Bruce. (Director/coscreenwriter). (2008). *Journey to Mecca: In the footsteps of Ibn Battutah* [Motion picture]. Toronto: SK Films.

Pitt, Ruth. (Executive producer). (2005, August). *An Islamic history of Europe* [Television broadcast]. London: BBC.

Virjee, Masuma. (Director). (2007). *313* [Motion picture]. U.K.: DayDream Films.

Yusuf, Sami. (2005, 1 January). *Al-Mu'allim* (The Teacher) [Music CD]. London: Awakening Worldwide.

Index

A

Abbasid dynasty, 38
Abdallah, 9
Abduh, Muhammad, 108
Abraham, 10, 74, 85, 94
Abū Bakr, 13, 14, 22, 23
Abyssinia, 2, 6
African Americans, 4
Afterlife, 66–68
Agha Khan, 40
Ahmad, 9
'Ā'ishah, 14, 16
al-Afghani, Jamal al-Din, 108
al-Ash'ari, Abū al-Hasan, 55
al-Azhar University, 39
al-Banna, Hasan, 110
al-Baqir, Muhammad, 33
al-Bukhārī, 27
al-Din Chishti, Khaja Mu'in, 48
Alexandrian philosophical school, 60–61
al-Fārābī, Abū Nasr, 58
al-Ghazālī, Abu Hāmid Muhammad ibn Muhammad at-Tūsī, 62
al-Hallāj, Mansūr, 43
al-Hujjah, Muhammad al-Mahdī, 35
'Alī, 13, 15, 17, 30, 32, 35, 36, 55, 95

selected sayings of, 33–34
Ali, Muhammad, 107
'Alī ibn Abī Tālib. See 'Alī
al-Jīlānī, Abd al-Qādir, 98
al-Khwārizmī, Muhammad ibn Mūsā, 61
al-Kindī, Yaqūb ibn Ishāq as-Sabah, 58
Allah, 7, 46, 63
al-Lat, 7
al-Madīnah, 14
Almsgiving. See Zakah
al-Musta'li, 39
al-Muttalib, 'Abd, 9
al-Nabi, Madinat, 14
al-Nasir, Gamal Abd, 109
al-Qadir, Abd, 107
al-Qaeda, 110
al-Sādiq, 35
al-'Uzza, 7
al-Wahhab, Muhammad ibn Abd, 108
Amina, 9
Angelic agency, 66
Ansar, 13
Arabia
  before Islam, 5
  religions in, 6–8
  socioeconomic structure, 5–6
  in the seventh century CE, 2

Arabian Jews, 6
Arabic language, 20, 83
Arabs, 4
  before Islam, 5
Arafat plain, 74
Ar-Rūmī, Jalāl ad-Din, 47, 50
Asceticism, 44
Ash'ariyya theological school,
    55–57
  human reason, 57
As-Sādiq, Ja'far, 35, 102
Ataturk, Mustafa Kemal, 109
Ayat, 22
Ayatollah Khomeini, 31

Baath Party, 31
Bahá'í faith, 29
Batin, 38
Ben Bella, 109
Bosnia, 3
Brahmins, 44
Breath control, *zikr* exercise, 46
Buddha, 44
Buddhism, 65
Byzantine Empire, 2, 6

C

Cairo, 38
Caliphs, 15
Calligraphy, 80, 83–84
Central Asia, 4
Charity. *See Zakah*
Chisthi order, 48
Christianity, 44, 65
Christian population, 6
Circumcision

female circumcision, 86
  male circumcision, 85–86
Conversion to Islam, 69
Coptic Christians, 86
Cyclical time concept, 38

D

Da'i, 35
Death, 91–92
Dhikr. See *Zikr*
Dhu'l-Hijja (Zu'l-Hijja), 94
Divine Hadith (Hadith Qudsi), 26
Divine unity, 63–64
Divorce, 90–91

E

Egypt, 86
Eid al-Adha (hajj), 94
Eid al-Fitr, 72, 93–94
E-jihad, 111
Eschatology, 66
Europe, Eastern, 4
European societies, 107
Europeanization, 108

Falsafa, 53
Fana, 43–44
Faqihs, 105
Farewell Pilgrimage, 14
Fasting, 71–72
Fātima, 13, 33, 39
Fatimid dynasty, 38
Fatwas, 105
Fiqh, 100
Funerals, 92–93

G

Gabriel, 12, 66
Gaozu raid, 8
Ghijduvani, 49
Great Emigration. *See* Hijra
Greater Occultation, 37

H

Hadith, 11, 19, 24–26, 37
  collections, 27
  as history, 26
Hafsa, 23, 24
Hagar, 73
Hajj (pilgrimage), 73–75
Halima, 10
Hanafi school, 102, 104
Hanbali school, 102
Hasan (beautiful), 26
Hāshim clan, 9
Heaven, 67, 68
Hell, 67
Hellenistic philosophy, 60
Hijab, 89
Hijra, 12–14
Hijri calendar, 93
Hinduism, 44, 65
Husayn (Hasan), 17, 32, 33
Hussein, Saddam, 31

I

Iblis, 66
Ibn 'Affān, 'Uthmān, 15, 23, 24
Ibn al-Hajjāj, Muslim, 27
Ibn al-Haytham, Abū 'Alī
  al-Hasan, 61
Ibn Hanbal, Ahmad, 27, 104

Ibn Marwān, 'Abd al-Malik, 24
Ibn Sīnā, Abū 'Alī al-Husayn ibn
  'Abd Allāh, 58–59, 61
Ijtihad, 30, 37, 104
Imam, 32, 35
iMuslims, 111
India, 4, 48, 108
  Naqshbandi order in, 49
Indian Muslims, 4
Indonesia, 2, 4
Iran, 31
  Islamic revolution, 109
Iraq, 31
Ishmael, 73, 94
Islam
  birth of, 1–2
  conversion to, 69
  definition of, 1
  modern. *See* Modernity
  texts, 19–28. *See also* Qur'an
Islamic feminism, 110
Islamic law, 99–100
  and call to prayer, 103
  faqihs, 105
  fatwas, 105
  muftis, 105
  principles of jurisprudence,
    102–104
  sources, 99–100
Islamic mystical poetry, 41
Islamic republic, 109
Islamic religious holidays, 93–96
  Dhu'l-Hijja (Zu'l-Hijja), 94
  Eid al-Adha (Hajj), 94
  Eid al-Fitr, 93–94
  Muharram, 95–96
Islamic Revolution, in Iran, 109
Islamic Salvation Front, Algeria,
  110

Ismā'īl, 35, 37
Ismā'īlis sect, 35, 37–40
Isnad, 26

Jabriyya, 54
Ja'fari, 35
Jamaat-i Islam, 110
Jesus, 44, 64, 65
Jihad (striving), 31, 75–77, 110
Judaism, 65
Judge, in pre-Islamic Arabia, 8

K

Ka'ba, 9, 10, 14, 15, 73
Kalam (theology), 53–54
Khadija, 5, 10–12, 88
Khaled, Amr, 111
Khan, Nusrat Fateh Ali, 48
Khawarij, 54
Koran. *See* Qur'an
Kufic script, 83

L

Lebanon, 96
Legal status of women, 86–87
Lesser Occultation, 37

M

Mahmud II, 107
Malaysia, 85
Maliki school, 102
Manāt, 7
Marriage, 57–59
  as legal contract, 89–90
Marwa, 73

Masjid. See Mosque
Masjid al-Haram, 10
Masnavī-ye Ma'navī, 47
Mawdudi, Abu al-Ala, 110
Mecca, 1, 9,
Medieval Muslims, 61
Medina, 1, 14
Mevlevi order, 49–51
Mevlevis, 47
Middle East, 31
Mihrab, 82
Modern Islam. *See* Islam, modern
Modernity, 2
  twentieth century, 108-111
  twenty-first century, 111
Monotheism, 68
Morocco, 2
Moslems. *See* Muslims
Mosque, 55–57
Mu'āwiyah, 15, 17, 32
Muftis, 105
Muhajirs, 13
Muhammad, 1, 53, 64, 86
  birth of, 9
  childhood, 9–10
  emigration of, 12–14
  encounter with Gabriel, 12
  marriage to Khadija, 10–12
  multiple wives, 87
  Ummah after, 15–18
Muhammadiyya movement, 108
Muharram, 95–96
Mu'inuddin Chishti, 98
Mujahidin, 110
Mujtahid, 104
Multiple wives, 87–89
Murji'a, 54
Musa, 35
Muslim Brotherhood, 110
Muslims, 1, 13

as Arab descent, 4
in United States, 3
Musnod ibn Hanbal, 104
Mu'tazila theological school, 55–57
    human reason, 57
Mystical Islam. *See* Sufism

ℵ

Nahj al-Balaghah, 33
Namaz, 70–71
Naqshband, Baha al-Din, 48
Naqshbandi order, 48–49
Nass, 35, 37
New Testament, 65
Nizar, 39
Nizari Ismā'īli community, 40
North Africa, 108
Northern Africa, 4
Nowruz, 93
Nurbakhshia sect, 29

O

Ottomans, 31, 47, 51, 83

P

Pakistan, 96
Persia, 6
Philosophy, 57–59
Pilgrimage, 73–75
Pillars of Faith, 63–68
    afterlife, 66–68
    angelic agency, 66
    divine unity, 63–64
    prophecy, 64
    revelation, 65–66
Pillars of Practice, 68–75
    hajj (pilgrimage), 73–75

salah (prayer), 70–71
sawm (fasting), 71–72
shahada, 68–69
zakah (almsgiving), 72–73
Poetry, in pre-Islamic Arabia, 7
Political independence, 109
Political Islam, 110
Polygyny, 88
Prayer, 70–71, 79, 103
Principles of jurisprudence,
    102–104
Prophecy, 64
Prophets, 38
Psalms, 65

Q

Qadariyya, 54
Qadis, 105
Qasimshahis, 40
Qavvali, 48
Qur'an, 11, 15, 17, 19–24, 53, 54,
    55–56, 65, 68, 70–71, 88, 99,
    102, 110
    ayat, 22
    compilation, 22–24
    suras, 21–22
Quraysh tribe, 9

R

Rābi'ah al-'Adawīyah, 42
Radicalism, 109
Rak'ah, 70
Ramadan, 71–72, 93–94
Reconquista, 17
Revelation, 65–66
Rightly Guided Caliphs, 16
Rites. *See specific rituals*
Rituals, similarity across countries, 4

Rock of Alamut, 40
Rumi. *See* Jalāl ad-Din ar-Rūmī

S

Safa, 73
Sahih (sound), 26
Saints, 98
Sama, 51
Sasanid dynasty, 2, 60
Sasanid Persia, 6
Sawing *zikr. See Zikr*
Sawm (fasting), 71–72
Sayyida Nafisa, 98
Schools of thought
  Jabriyya, 54
  Khawarij, 54
  Murji'a, 54
  Qadariyya, 54
Scientific discoveries, 61
Scientific literature, 60
Sects. *See* Bahaism sect; Ismā'īlis
    sect; Nurbakhshia sect; Shi'a
    sect; Sufism; Sunni sect;
    Wahhabiya sect; Zaydis sect
Seljuk dynasty, 50
Senegal, 2
Shafi'i school, 102, 104
Shahada, 68–69
Shams al-Din, 47
Sharia, 102. *See also* Islamic law
Shi'a Imams, 32–33
Shi'a sect, 17, 27, 29, 30–32, 66
  marriage law, 87
  Prayer of Kumayl (Du'a Kumayl),
    36
Shirk, 67
Shrine cults, 97
Siddhārtha Gautama, 44

Silsila-yi Khajagan ("Chain of
    Masters"), 48
Sirhindī, Ahmad, 49
Socioeconomic structure, before
    Islam, 5–6
Soothsayer, in pre-Islamic Arabia,
    7–8
South Arabia, 2
Soviet Union, 97
Spain, 17
Sufism, 40
  Chisthi order, 48
  Mevlevi order, 49–50
  Naqshbandi order, 48–49
  orders, 46–48
  origins of, 41–43
  path of, 44–45
  shrine, 98
  Sufi orders, 40–41
  union with God concept,
    43–44
  zikr (meditation), 45–46
Sunna, 25, 27–28, 102
Sunni sect, 17, 24, 29–30, 66
  jurists schools, 102
  marriage law, 87
Suras, 21–22

T

Tālib, Abu, 10
Tariqas, 46
Tariqa-yi Muhammadiya ("Path of
    Muhammad"), 49
*Ta'ziyah*s, 96
Telli Baba, 98
Texts, Islamic. *See* Islamic texts
Theology, 53–54
Thulth (thuluth) script, 83

Torah, 65
Tribal and clan interactions, 8
Tughras, 83
Turkey, 31, 85
Twelvers, 35–37, 66, 70, 102

𝓤

'Umar, 15, 22
Umayyad dynasty, 16, 54
Ummah, 4, 99
   after Muhammad, 15–18
Umra, 73
Union with God, 43–44
United States
   Muslims in, 4
Usul al-fiqh, 100

𝓦

Wahhabiya sect, 29
Wakil (envoys), 37
Westernization, 108

Whirling Dervishes, 47, 49
Women, 110
   hijab, 89
   legal status of, 86–87
Wudu (*wuzu*), 70

𝓨

Yathrib, 12, 13, 14
Yazīd, 17

𝐙

Zahir, 38
Zakah (almsgiving), 68, 72–73
Zamzam, 73
Zayd, 33
Zayd ibn Thābit, 23
Zaydi imam, 35
Zaydis sect, 34–35
Zikr (meditation), 45–46
Zoroastrian, 6
Zu'l-hijja, 73

 # About the Author

*J*amal J. Elias is Chair of the Department of Religious Studies and Class of 1965 Endowed Term Professor at the University of Pennsylvania. He has written and lectured widely on the Qur'an, Sufism, and religion and material culture across the Islamic world. He is the author of numerous books on Islam and Islamic society, including *Key Themes for the Study of Islam* (Oneworld, 2010), *On Wings of Diesel: Trucks, Identity and Culture in Pakistan* (Oneworld, 2010), *Islam* (Prentice Hall and Routledge, 1999), *Death Before Dying: Sufi Poems of Sultan Bahu* (University of California Press, 1998), and *The Throne Carrier of God: The Life and Thought of 'Ala' ad-dawla as-Simnani* (SUNY Press, 1995).

BERKSHIRE ENCYCLOPEDIA OF WORLD HISTORY 2ND EDITION

Editors: **William H. McNeill,** *University of Chicago,* **Jerry H. Bentley,** *University of Hawaii, Manoa,* **David Christian,** *Macquarie University,* **Ralph C. Croizier,** *University of Victoria,* **J. R. McNeill,** *Georgetown University*

> *Library Journal* Best Reference Source
> *Booklist* Editor's Choice
> *Choice* Outstanding Academic Title

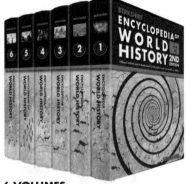

This landmark work has grown from 5 to 6 volumes and includes over 100 new articles on environmental history, world art, global communications, and information technology, as well as updates on recent events such as the Sichuan and Haiti earthquakes and the global economic crisis. Hundreds of new illustrations enhance visual appeal, while updated Further Reading sections guide readers toward continued study.

6 VOLUMES
978-1-933782-65-2
Price: US$875
3,200 pages • 8½ × 11"

"A masterful title that weaves together social, scientific, anthropological, and geographical influences on world history, this set will be the benchmark against which future history encyclopedias are compared...[it] belongs on the shelves of all high-school, public, and academic libraries. In short: buy it. Now."
—*Booklist* starred review of the first edition

BERKSHIRE ENCYCLOPEDIA OF WORLD SPORT 2ND EDITION

Presenting everything and anything you want to know about sports and the sporting life, this single reference resource captures the essence of the world of sport and its incredible variety. Comprehensive, illustrated articles, updated and expanded, offer full coverage of all the social and human issues in sports that keep talk radio buzzing—the background and low-down for fans and students alike. Coverage begins with sport among prehistoric hunter-gatherers and extends to the global sports industry of the twenty-first century.

5 VOLUMES
978-1-933782-67-6
Price: US$595
2,700 pages • 8½ × 11"

"[The *Berkshire Encyclopedia of World Sport*] is a completely fresh work. It is a fine addition to any library at the high-school level or above."
—*Booklist* starred review of the first edition

BERKSHIRE ENCYCLOPEDIA OF CHINA

MODERN AND HISTORIC COVERAGE OF THE WORLD'S NEWEST AND OLDEST GLOBAL POWER

宝库山 中华全书: 跨越历史和现代 审视最新和最古老的全球大国

China is changing our world, and Berkshire Publishing, known for its acclaimed encyclopedias on a wide array of global issues including the acclaimed 6-volume *Encyclopedia of Modern Asia*, is proud to publish the first major resource designed for students, teachers, businesspeople, government officials, and tourists seeking a greater understanding of China today.

"Take a publisher with a decade of experience in China, add a group of well-known Chinese and Western scholars, pay special attention to details (each of the 800 articles begins on its own page, all article titles are rendered in English, Chinese characters, and transliterations), add 1100 unique photographs, sprinkle in dozens of traditional Chinese proverbs, do it all on recycled, chlorine-free paper, throw in a year of free online access, and the end result is this sumptuous resource on all things China for the 21st century."

—*Library Journal* Best Reference 2009

5 VOLUMES
978-0-9770159-4-8
Price: US$675
2,754 pages • 8½ × 11"

BERKSHIRE DICTIONARY OF CHINESE BIOGRAPHY

宝库山 中华傳記字典

Editor-in-chief: **Kerry Brown**, *Chatham House, London*
Advisory Board: **Christopher Cullen**, *University of Cambridge*, **Julia Lovell**, *University of London*, **Guoxiang Peng**, *Tsinghua University*, **Chloe Starr**, *University of Oxford*, **Roel Sterckx**, *University of Cambridge*, **Jan Stuart**, *British Museum*, **John Wills Jr.**, *University of Southern California*, and **Frances Wood**, *British Library*

Chinese history can be overwhelming, and no one claims to understand in detail more than specific periods of this great sweep of political, social, and economic development. But the world's leading China scholars can, together, tell us the whole story. The *Berkshire Dictionary of Chinese Biography* will make this immense history manageable—easier to comprehend and digest—by taking the reader through it in the life stories of key figures who have shaped, influenced, and transformed China. These individuals include emperors, politicians, poets, writers, artists, scientists, explorers, and philosophers.

3 VOLUMES
978-1-933782-66-9
Price: US$595
1,840 pages • 8½ × 11"

BERKSHIRE ENCYCLOPEDIA OF SUSTAINABILITY

10 VOLUMES

978-1-933782-01-0

Price: US$1500

Discounts available

8½×11"

A ground-breaking interdisciplinary resource for 21st-century students and professionals, providing the knowledge and solutions we need to transform our common future. Over 1,200 expert contributors from many academic fields and from across the globe add to a comparative, cross-cultural approach, including different points of view and important debates.

"With the charge to inform and to represent multiple perspectives, the writers of this thoughtfully produced volume stay on topic and handily present the relationship between their subject and the overall concept of sustainability."

— *School Library Journal* review of *The Spirit of Sustainability*